Investment Beliefs

Investment Beliefs

A Positive Approach to Institutional Investing

Kees Koedijk
Professor of Financial Management at the Tilburg School of Economics and Management, Tilburg University, The Netherlands

Alfred Slager
Chief Investment Officer, Stork Pension Fund; Tilburg School of Economics and Management

First published 2011 by
PALGRAVE MACMILLAN

Palgrave Macmillan in the UK is an imprint of Macmillan Publishers Limited, registered in England, company number 785998, of Houndmills, Basingstoke, Hampshire RG21 6XS.

Palgrave Macmillan in the US is a division of St Martin's Press LLC, 175 Fifth Avenue, New York, NY 10010.

Palgrave Macmillan is the global academic imprint of the above companies and has companies and representatives throughout the world.

Palgrave® and Macmillan® are registered trademarks in the United States, the United Kingdom, Europe and other countries

ISBN 978-1-349-33009-6   ISBN 978-0-230-30757-5 (eBook)
DOI 10.1057/9780230307575

This book is printed on paper suitable for recycling and made from fully managed and sustained forest sources. Logging, pulping and manufacturing processes are expected to conform to the environmental regulations of the country of origin.

A catalogue record for this book is available from the British Library.

A catalogue record for this book is available from the Library of Congress.

10   9   8   7   6   5   4   3   2   1
20   19   18   17   16   15   14   13   12   11

Contents

List of Tables

List of Figures

Foreword

Investment Beliefs and Tomorrow's Pension Fund

The late 1960s were auspicious times to trade the pursuit of a PhD degree in economics for a career in the institutional investing business. Terms such as Modern Portfolio Theory (MPT) and the Efficient Markets Hypothesis (EMH) had just entered the investment lexicon. My first job in the business was two-fold: 1) understand how a 'real world' institutional investment shop operates, and 2) see if the ideas behind concepts such as MPT and the EMH have any practical relevance in the real world of institutional investing. By the mid-1970s, I had accomplished both tasks (at least to my own satisfaction) and was ready for the next challenge.

That next challenge arrived through a little book by management philosopher Peter Drucker, which he would describe twenty years later as his least-read and most prescient. *The Unseen Revolution* (1976) provided the broader context in which to assess the relevance not only of the ideas behind MPT and EMH, but also of institutional investing as it was practised at that time. The central question Drucker posed was how, and in whose interest, the coming wave of retirement savings would be managed. He observed that ordinary workers were on their way to becoming owners of the means of production not through a Marxian revolution, but through pension plan membership. He worried, however, that this vast pool of financial capital would end up being managed not in workers' interests, but in the interests of politicians, corporate executives, labor leaders, and the financial services industry.

Back in 1976, Drucker's central question and his related agency concerns struck me as profoundly important to the future of not only institutional investing, but also to the future of capitalism itself. And that continues to be my view today, as I research, write, and speak on "Tomorrow's Pension Fund", with its five critical success drivers: 1) aligned interests, 2) good governance, 3) right-scaled, 4) competitive compensation, and 5) sensible investment beliefs. Stating the obvious about the fifth success driver, managing a pension fund without sensible investment beliefs is likely to be as successful as circumventing the globe without a compass (or a GPS).

Given that this entire book is about sensible investment beliefs, this foreword is no place to address the topic in any detail. I would be amiss, however, not to acknowledge another intellectual giant who has greatly influenced my own thinking on the topic. John Maynard Keynes' 1936 opus *The General*

Theory of Employment, Interest, and Money was mainly about the respective roles of fiscal and monetary policies in stabilizing capitalist economies at high rates of employment. Yet in my view, Chapter 12, titled "The State of Long Term Expectations", still stands as one of the greatest essays ever written on the topic of investment beliefs in an institutional investment context.

Keynes observed that institutional investing often seems to resemble a beauty contest. However, the goal of the contest is not to pick the most beautiful stock by some objective standard, but to pick the stock average opinion will deem the most beautiful "three months or one year hence". In Keynes' view, such a mindset fosters short-termism and mind games at the expense of thoughtfully converting precious savings into long-term, wealth-creating investments. I encountered the same mindset when I began to study institutional investment practices as an insider some forty years ago. Unfortunately, this same mindset continues to hold sway in far too many cases today.

Why has change been so difficult? It is hard to better Keynes' 1936 explanation even today. In his words: "Wordly wisdom teaches that it is better for reputation to fail conventionally than to succeed unconventionally". In other words, if everybody else is playing the beauty contest game, you'd better play it too. It is far safer to be wrong in a crowd than to be wrong and alone. So how do we move institutional investing from this zero-sum to a positive-sum game? That is where the other four Tomorrow's Pension Fund success drivers come in. The world needs more arms-length, large-scale pension funds with great governance and operations capabilities. These are the funds capable of not only articulating sensible investment beliefs, but also capable of using them to create value for their stakeholders.

So we commend Kees Koedijk and Alfred Slager for taking on the challenge to write this book on sensible investment beliefs. It has much to offer those ready to receive its messages. Peter Drucker and John Maynard Keynes would be pleased.

Keith Ambachtsheer

Acknowledgements

This book did not materialize overnight; a succession of articles, present-
ations and papers shaped our thinking over the years, inspired by first hand
experience, sharing dilemmas and insights with trustees, investment
managers and regulators.

Kees Koedijk served on numerous investment committees of pension
funds, helping trustees to further effective pension fund management. Kees
has published widely on pension funds and pension fund management.
Recently, he initiated the website "global pension survey" (www.global-
pensionsurvey.com) which surveys global pension leaders on a quarterly
basis.

Alfred Slager had the good fortune to work at pension fund PGGM (now
PFZW), an organization committed to continually improving its investment
philosophy and challenging commonly accepted ideas in asset management,
where Else Bos and Jaap van Dam, and Leo Lueb were an important source of
inspiration, generously taking time to debate many of the topics outlined in
this book, definitely enhancing the quality of this book. The debates with
Gerard Rutten of DSM Pension Services were equally inspiring, firmly embedding the investment management topics within the pension sector.

We both have benefited tremendously from numerous discussions with
trustees, giving courses or serving on pension funds' investment committees,
helping shape the ideas into applicable frameworks. We were also fortunate
to discuss our research and findings at several seminars. Especially the International Centre for Pension Management (ICPM) provided a stimulating platform to discuss our ideas with the top professionals in the pension sector,
where special thanks go to Keith Ambachtsheer and Don Raymond.

Caroline Studdert moulded the first draft into a readable and accessible
book. We thank Robert van der Meer, Ronald Wuijster, Roeli van Wijk and
Keith Ambachtsheer for their invaluable feedback. Anouk Akkermans, Bart
Verheijden and Joost de Bakker provided skillful research assistance, while
Anja Schellekens and Frieda Rikkers instilled sorely needed project manage-
ment discipline, preventing us from drifting off from time to time.

1
Introduction

Trustees, investment managers and professionals in the pension sector should read this book. Not because we would be pleased with higher sales, but because we think we have something to say to help them manage their investments better. And this is sorely needed. Pension funds and endowments are currently experiencing a rough ride. Since 2000, three major financial crises have taken a large chunk out of the wealth of pension funds, at a time when we increasingly depend on pension funds for our future welfare.

Pension funds, mutual funds and insurance companies in the United States manage assets worth $30 trillion; worldwide, this amounts to $67 trillion. For most citizens in the developed economies, the wealth invested in their pension makes these assets – next to their home – the biggest they are likely to own in their lives. All over the world, governments are introducing new pension schemes to save for future retirement, trying to cope with ageing societies.

Investment strategies that seemed sound are now unhinged. Investment risks that were considered too improbable have occurred. In a striking anecdote, James Picerno (1998), author of the CapitalSpectator weblog,[1] recalls a meeting on the future of investment management. Pointing to an abstract, unmarked graph that depicted a line rising from the bottom-left to the top-right corner, one speaker declared that whether it was assets under management, market indices, the number of investment consultants, fees, or any number of the measures of the business, the graph said it all – they go up. The audience laughed in 1998 but would probably not appreciate the humor today. The fallout of the financial crisis has wiped billions of dollars off the balance sheets of banks, institutional investors and consumers. The crisis also raises questions that hit at the heart of finance and investments. Should investors stick to equities after the 50% drop in 2008, and assume a recovery is on the way? Is the past the best predictor of the future and will most of the losses be compensated in a few years? In other words, how much "business as usual" can we assume?

Risk management fares no better. Pension funds have made great advances, creating an elaborate system of risk management indicators based on Peter Drucker's adage: "What gets measured gets managed". Investors have constructed an elaborate toolkit for this purpose, introducing eloquent terms like Value at Risk, tracking error and information ratio.

But Peter Drucker's recipe for corporate financial management cannot easily be translated to financial markets. At end-2007, many European pension funds had ample cover ratios, indicating assets comfortably higher than future pension payouts, and – based on the risk models – a negligible chance of running the risk that the cover ratio would fall below the required minimum set by the regulator. But by end-2008, the negligible had become impossible to ignore; almost all pension funds fell below the minimum. The relative comfort that trustees had derived from risk management models has been pulverized. Risk management has since been expanded to include the concept of the "Black Swan" (Taleb 2005): events that are thought of as improbable but actually have a high probability of occurring or recurring.

At the same time, the pressure to excel is greater than ever, especially since asset management is all about delivering the better mousetrap: higher investment returns. Managers now seek new beacons to illuminate the path of their investment strategies. As a result, a profound shift is taking place in the paradigm governing the management of pension funds (Ambachtsheer 2005). The shift is away from static investment policies, supported by static beliefs about return distributions in general and about the equity risk premium in particular. Instead, there is increasing acceptance that return distributions are only partially predictable, that previously accepted guidelines and truisms in investments are open to debate, that a (self) assessment of investment behavior matters as much as crafting quantitative models, and that proactive informed investors can in fact positively impact investment outcomes through their actions.

This realization in turn has profound implications for how pension funds should design their business models and their investment functions. Many people attribute the success of firms like eBay and Amazon to the way they are using new technologies not just to make their operations more efficient but to create completely new business models (e.g. Gurley 2001). Does something similar apply to pension funds? To succeed, pension funds must have a clear idea of where they do and do not add value in the capital markets.

Having the right investment beliefs and putting them into practice is key to delivering the right results. That's the main message of our book.

Asset managers should worry less about the stocks and products they pick for their clients and more about getting their investment beliefs right. After a steep decline in the global stock markets and a recovery that is still uncertain, surviving in the asset management industry is probably one of the toughest challenges around. All that counts in the end are the investment returns you achieve for your client, whether this is a private client or a pension fund. Most asset managers do not measure up to the broad market performance and constantly risk being acquired by other asset managers or abandoned by their clients. In this cut-throat industry, it is simply is not enough to have a good organization, good staff and a well-defined and embedded mission. You need to go soul-searching and formulate your own investment beliefs: a clear view on how you perceive the way capital markets work, and how your organization can add value and strive for excellence.

CEOs of companies are by now probably shrugging their shoulders and saying: so what else is new? Soul-searching, formulating your added value to customers and society – pretty basic elements. We argue that this is not the case in the pension fund industry, perhaps even in the investment management industry. There is an army of analysts, researchers and investors out there to search for new anomalies in financial markets, and structure and mould them into investment strategies.

But somewhere along the way the bigger picture – do we actually need these new strategies – has blurred. That's where our book steps in.

Our research shows that pension funds that make clear choices about how they view the financial markets, which way they add value and how to implement this, tend to earn consistently higher returns. Funds have an array of choices at their disposal to add value. Earning excess returns in financial markets, focusing on costs, searching for niche strategies to improve risk, reducing costs, improving return-risk profiles of the investments – that's just a selection of the fundamental choices to be made. A 1% differential per year can easily be the decisive factor in becoming a winner or loser in the pension fund industry in 2020.

Investment results will ultimately determine the long-term success of pension funds and institutional investors. If trustees are more effective, they can make a real difference to the future for their clients or participants, but to be effective, it is necessary to understand how the investment process works and what the real drivers behind failure or success are. Real drivers are investment beliefs: views on how the capital markets work and whether to take an active stance on this. Formulating investment beliefs helps with managing funds better, with getting an effective grip on external managers, and with governance with participants.

A key upfront message is: Think twice about your investment philosophy. Managing your investment portfolio entails more than determining an asset mix and monitoring it regularly, and a good investment process is an essential building block for well-governed funds. Funds today should not restrict themselves to fine-tuning their investment process; they also need to adapt to changing environments. Clearly formulated investment beliefs help in making this transition.

1.1   Synopsis

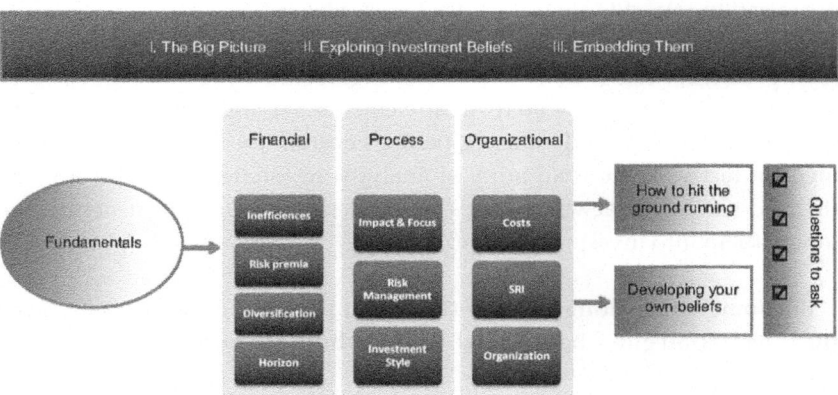

Figure 1.1   Set up of the book

Part I begins by painting the big picture. Articulation of investment beliefs and an investment philosophy not only provides the right underpinnings for asset allocation, but is also an integral part of the governance of the investment organization. The pension fund has to balance different interests. Pensioners and regulators increasingly demand more clarity as the invested assets accumulate further. The investment organization on the other hand has to determine its added value, realizing that it is a pension investor, not an asset manager.

Part II presents a useful and readily applicable overview of what these investment beliefs are; we show how asset managers use them. We examine investment beliefs from the world's leading fund managers, pension plans and endowment funds. These are the companies that appear on everybody's short list when buying asset management services, and are viewed as excellent companies in the asset management industry. Together they provide a broad based and coherent picture of today's state of the art views on asset management. The survey spans North American and European companies, where the world's assets are concentrated.

We then cluster these investment views and search for commonalities. We purge our analysis by asking ourselves: is this investment belief practically applicable, and does it make sense in light of the state of finance and investments today? Our analysis suggests that managers with well-developed investment beliefs tend to show better results. We analyze and identify which investments beliefs have a strong effect on performance. We then show how managers can use these investment beliefs to sharpen the competitive edge of their companies. With the three groups of investment beliefs we unearthed, we identify promising strategies for the future: *capital markets* strategy, *organization skills* strategy and *society* strategy. We present practical examples of how asset managers can use these strategies to their advantage.

Part III homes in on execution. We confront managers in the financial services industry with a thought-provoking question: Are their asset management organizations really looking at the right things? Are their organizations attuned to a set of investment beliefs that can stand the test of time and argued debate? Do they also help direct the organization's resources to exploit the investment opportunities they believe in? These questions are at the same time the reasons why asset management companies should have these explicit beliefs. They promote transparency in goals and implementation, benefiting investors, boards of trustees and the manager. We also provide a checklist for pension fund managers on what to do when their organizations have no explicitly defined investment beliefs, but are keen to develop them for future success.

Finally, a word on how to read this book. Unlike a suspense novel, you can read the book from back to front just as easily as from front to back. If you're in the midst of discussions on investment philosophy, investment beliefs, or just the evaluation of the investment plan, simply go to the table of contents, find a specific topic that interests you, and jump in. Chances are that you've picked something from Part II. This book leverages the research of many top-flight academics. This helps trustees and investments professionals get up to speed with the latest debates in investment management, and ask the right questions. We provide an accessible overview that saves reading a lot of journals and books and attending endless seminars.

Readers expecting in-depth debates on the merits of specific theories and ideas might be disappointed. Also, we do not intend to compete with handbooks around that provide investors and trustees with exhaustive details on investment management.[2] We focus on the *fundamentals* of investment management, and humbly build on the vast literature delving into specific strategies, investment styles and instruments. We only refer to academic debates if they directly affect how funds should or could be managed, but we also pepper the text with notes and references for readers who would like to acquire more background.

Part I

Investment Beliefs: The Fundamentals

Part 1

Investment Basics: The Fundamentals

2
Think Twice About Your Investment Philosophy

Summary

✓ Managing your investment portfolio entails more than determining an asset mix and monitoring it regularly.

✓ Only a minority of funds currently devotes sufficient time to formulating Investment Beliefs and actually understands investment principles.

✓ The formulation of Investment Beliefs contributes to performance, as it helps trustees and investment managers to make informed decisions consistent with their objectives.

✓ Funds today should not limit themselves to fine-tuning their investment processes (execution), but should also adapt to changing environments. Investment Beliefs help in this transition.

Strangely enough, the extent to which performance is related to investment management attributes or characteristics is a largely unknown empirical question. Much attention is paid to investment management organizations and their products by market regulators, the media, institutional and retail investors, investment consultants and rating agencies (Gallagher 2003). But the research has largely concentrated on the measurement of portfolio performance and performance persistence; research with respect to the determinants of investment performance and the specific characteristics that differentiate manager returns is sparse.

Keith Ambachtsheer, a prominent consultant to and researcher of pension funds, strongly believes that thinking about the design of the investment organization pays off. In 2004, he analyzed the investment organizations of Harvard Management Company (HMC) and Ontario Teachers Pension Plan (OTPP) Board, both organizations renowned for their innovative investment policies and strong returns. HMC, which manages Harvard University's endowment, $26 billion at June 2009, outpaced the University's total return target and its internal benchmark, realizing an annualized rate of return of 11.7% over the last 20 years. Canadian pension fund OTPP, with $92 billion in assets at end-2009, realized an average annual rate of return of 9.7% from 1990, generating $19 billion more than its market benchmarks – almost one-quarter of the fund's growth. We will revisit these funds later (see Case study 9.1).

Ambachtsheer (2004) asserts that the success of these funds has key elements in common: a legal foundation that clarifies stakeholder interests and minimizes the potential for agency conflicts, and a governance process that crystallizes the organization's mission and understands the critical elements needed to achieve it. Claude Lamoureux, Ontario's CEO in charge of the fund's transformation, put it more succinctly: run the fund like you run a business (Lamoureux 2008).

Harvard and Ontario are investment organizations with clear mandates and a well thought out governance process. These two elements are key to success. In a broader setting, Vittas, Impavido and O'Connor from the Worldbank (2008) have investigated public pension funds worldwide. They find that public pension funds benefit from low operating costs because they enjoy economies of scale and avoid large marketing costs. However, if investment performance lags behind, this important advantage has been dissipated. Weak governance structure, a lack of independence from government interference, and a low level of transparency and public accountability can all contribute to poor investment performance.

Even among countries where good governance practices are more institutionalized, differences in performance creep in. Clark and Urwin (2007) compare what they consider to be best practice pension funds with other funds, and find that the former generate an additional 1–2% per year. These are crucial return differences when return expectations are continually being downgraded in the light of recurrent financial crises. Urwin and Clark's research shows that best practice funds treat investments as a strategic core element, based on:

- Investment beliefs that can stand the tests of reason, informed debate, and occasional revision when new evidence comes to light.
- Investment processes that integrate stakeholder risk tolerances and investment beliefs using combinations of seasoned judgment and state-of-the-art financial engineering practices.

From the "birth" of management literature when Peters and Waterman wrote *In Search of Excellence* (1982), to *Good to Great* by Jim Collins (2001), the same message has resonated. Organizations that have a clear sense of their core competences deliver better results for their stakeholders. Why should this be any different for pension funds managing their investments? Investment beliefs are important because they create a context for value-creating investing. What are the core competencies of an investment organization aiming for success in the capital markets? How does and how should an institutional investor view capital markets? This is a strategic issue that seems obvious but has to date seldom been addressed in the literature (cf. Ambachtsheer 2004; Ambachtsheer and Ezra 1994). In a study of the global pension fund industry (cf. Ambachtsheer 2004; Ambachtsheer and Ezra 1994) the researchers find that elements including vision, strategic positioning and resource plan are significantly related to financial performance. The fourth factor is the asset allocation; long-term risk and return largely depends on how you compose and implement the portfolio.

2.1 Investment beliefs add value for trustees

If you are a trustee, have you ever wondered if you're on top of things? Are you a credible counterweight to the investment manager when he discusses the quarterly results for your fund, able to separate skill from luck? When new investment strategies are discussed, can you assess the risks and evaluate whether they really add value for the fund and its participants? These are just some of the questions trustees struggle with. In our conversations with trustees, a frequently raised question is: how on earth can a trustee manage an investment expert?

Gordon Clark, a prominent pension researcher in the UK, has surveyed the competence of British pension fund trustees. In the 2006 study, trustees' ability in solving problems relevant to their investment responsibilities is examined. The results show that trustees are more cautious with other peoples' money than with their own. The fact that trustees are not professionals has also led to concerns that trustees may lack the understanding to judge advice they receive from experts. Clark notes a growing tension between representation and expertise in several fields, using UK pension fund governance and the US mutual fund industries as examples. The evidence suggests that very few trustees have the competence and consistency of judgment to challenge the experts who are responsible for executing complex financial decisions.

The natural solution for tackling this gap between experts and trustees – if time and resources were available – would be for trustees to delve into the subjects at hand. Try to think like the asset manager is thinking, and get to the bottom of the latest derivative construction. But just as trustees are expert in their daily work, so is the investment manager. Swapping jobs isn't the answer. The answer lies in the fact that trustees need to look at the big picture as well the operational issues.

Any business faces two demands: it must execute its current activities in such a way as to survive today's challenges, and it must adapt these activities to survive tomorrow's. In a McKinsey study, Eric Beinhocker (2006) observes that since both executing and adapting require resources, managers face an unending competition for money, people and time to address the need to perform in the short run and the equally vital need to invest in the long run. Tom Peters and Bob Waterman are the writers of *In Search of Excellence* (1982), the seminal study on strategic management worldwide. They draw attention to this challenge and argue that organizations must be simultaneously "tight" in executing and "loose" in adapting.

Today's investment organizations also have to balance both. Organizations that are overly focused on execution create high barriers to adaptation for tomorrow. On the other hand, an organization with poor execution today has a slim chance of being around in the long term.

Improving execution: Formulating investment beliefs simplifies the task of both investment managers and pension fund trustees in evaluating investment management and strategies. If a fund does not have a coherent investment philosophy, trustees will find themselves rudderless and will become an

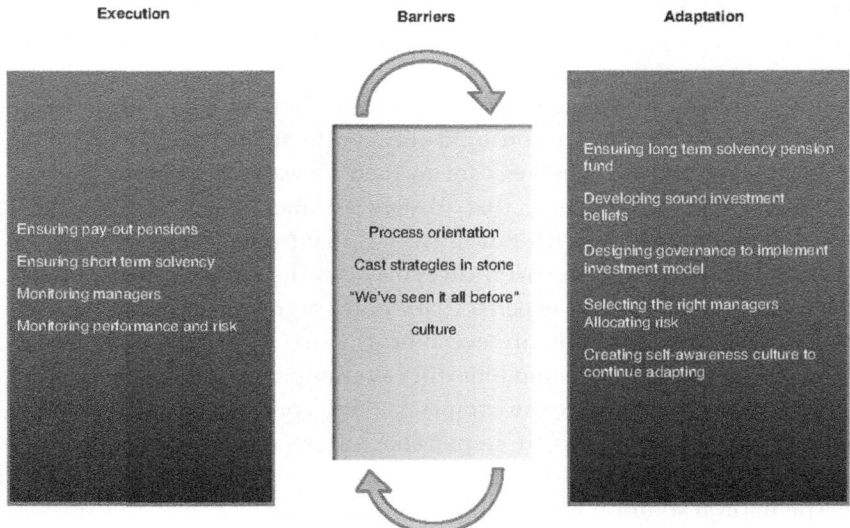

Execution	Barriers	Adaptation
Ensuring pay-out pensions	Process orientation	Ensuring long term solvency pension fund
Ensuring short term solvency	Cast strategies in stone	Developing sound investment beliefs
Monitoring managers	"We've seen it all before"	Designing governance to implement investment model
Monitoring performance and risk	culture	Selecting the right managers Allocating risk
		Creating self-awareness culture to continue adapting

Figure 2.1   Execution versus adaptation decisions for pension investors

easy prey to investment banks, consultants and asset managers each claiming to have found the magic strategy that beats the market. If you find this a ridiculous view, just think about the argument that John Bogle raises: asset manager costs have doubled from a 0.77% expense ratio in 1951 to 1.54% in 2007 for an average fund. When weighted by fund assets, the expense ratio rose from 0.60% to 0.87%, still an increase of nearly 50%. John Bogle, founder and former CEO of Vanguard, a large low-cost mutual fund group, has estimated that in the American financial sector, financial intermediation costs (ranging from marketing funds to managing assets and advising) added up to $528 billion in 2007 (Bogle 2008). On the one hand this is a tribute to the creativity of bankers and investment managers worldwide. But think about the implications. Have the returns of your fund or endowment risen by the same proportion? Probably not.

The investment management industry will probably shrug its shoulders and retort that costs are just a part of net returns, and that the sector has introduced an impressive suite of financial innovations to earn returns. However ... it probably never happened to your fund, but there are a lot of trustees out there who curse the day they started investing in alternatives, or portable alpha. And there are many more buzzwords around. Just think of Liability-Driven Investing, Exotic Beta, Value Investing, Socially Responsible Investment (SRI), Absolute Return Strategies, 130/30 Strategies, or fiduciary management (Table 2.1).

So the real challenge is to determine which innovations are relevant for a fund and why. Without a sound set of investment beliefs, a pension

Table 2.1   Innovations in investment management

	1980s	1990s	2000s
New Concepts	• Portfolio diversification	• Asset-liability management • International diversification • New risk tools (VaR, RVaR)	• Liability driven investments • Portfolio insurance • Risk budgeting • Absolute return investing • Alternative investing
New Instruments	• Derivatives • Private equity	• Currencies as an asset class • International investments	• Hedge funds • Catastrophe bonds • 130/30 strategies • Socially responsible investments (SRI)

fund might end up with a strategy that is not appropriate for its participants, given its objectives and its risk (aversion) profile. Clear beliefs also prevent a fund from switching from strategy to strategy and changing the portfolio more often than necessary, resulting in high transactions costs and eroding net investment results. With explicit investment beliefs, trustees and their investment managers can make informed decisions, instead of simply following the herd.

Improving adaptation: Just as companies compete for industry foresight and stake out a leadership position in the area of competence (Hamel and Prahalad 1994), asset managers have similar objectives within the investment management industry. Borrowing from Porter (1985), product leadership, customer intimacy and cost leadership are the main focus of company strategy. For investment managers, investment beliefs and their effective implementation form the cornerstone of their corporate strategies and thus their "unique selling proposition" for clients. In this respect, pension funds do not differ that much from other companies. You have to get to the core of your USP – unique selling proposition – to catch the imagination and earn the loyalty of your customer.

Companies that have a thorough understanding of their core USPs are also better prepared for the future. The supply side is constantly changing. Financial markets have become increasingly volatile since the 1970s, and financial innovation has flooded the market with new products and strategies. Similarly, trustees are also changing, which is a good thing. They do not accept any new product as the best solution around. In the *Financial Times*, consultants complained in several articles that they found it incomprehensible that trustees were not adopting the liability-driven investment model as the new best thing. The easy answer is that trustees are not up to the challenge. The better answer might well be that that many trustees have an intuitive feeling about their own USPs and the model does not seem to sit comfortably with this.

There might be a hunch about the fund's true USPs, but that's not the same as a set of explicit beliefs. A study by investment consultant Watson Wyatt in 2007 showed that fewer than half of UK pension fund trustees had given any thought to the investment beliefs that should be the basis of their investment strategy.[1] The survey asked trustees representing £80 billion in assets whether they had devoted as much as half a day to defining their investment beliefs, and 56% said they had not – which means that they have failed to consider the theoretical framework within which they make strategic investment decisions.

Other surveys do not present a rosier picture. In a 2005 survey for the *Engaged Investor* magazine of trustees of FTSE 350 company schemes, only 32% believed that they understood investment principles "very well". One in seven did not know their plan's investment benchmark (Robinson and Kakabadse, quoted in Boeri et al. 2006). The following parts of this section will outline the fundamentals of investment principles and beliefs and argue that this is not just a management fad – it's an effective tool to help you come to grips with the complexities of the financial markets.

3
Uncovering Beliefs

Summary

✓ Investing theory has been evolving rapidly since the 1950s and has undergone several paradigm shifts since the 1970s.

✓ Investment management is not a "hard science" as there are no absolute truths and certainties.

✓ Investment beliefs consist of four main elements: basic beliefs and beliefs related to theory, strategy and the organization. Determination and implementation of all four elements is necessary to have a workable Investment Beliefs set in place.

✓ An investment philosophy – a set of investment beliefs – should be dynamic, and the beliefs complementary, to ensure it adds value.

✓ The chances of developing a coherent set of Investment Beliefs are only credible when this is embedded within the broader governance of the fund.

✓ Various studies indicate that superior performance is linked to strong governance.

3.1 Viewpoints

Investors and trustees pronounce, act on or ignore investment beliefs on a daily basis, sometimes at their own peril. To illustrate this, we have collected a few quotations that we have picked up when meeting with trustees and advisors of pension funds for our research. We caught them at a bad time; in October and November 2008, bungee-jumping without a cord made more sense than investing in the stock markets, with losses racking up to 30% in the equity markets.

Trustee 1: "This is such an exceptional situation that the best thing is to do nothing"
His real thoughts: we've prepared for 98% of all possible cases, but now that we're in unchartered waters, we realize that we have no backup plan.

Trustee 2: "Stocks have decreased so dramatically, we should consider postponing rebalancing of the strategic portfolio for the time being"
His real thoughts: even though we have had thorough discussions about loss, now that we're experiencing it, the loss simply hurts too much. We've abandoned hope that equities will rebound and earn decent returns. We're entering a new paradigm, although we're not sure what it is.

Trustee 3: "We should keep faith in the long-term prospects of equities"
His real thoughts probably coincide with H. G. Wells' remark that today's crisis is tomorrow's joke. Yes, this is extreme, and hitherto unknown, but as an article of faith, I'd like to stick to the merits of long-term investing and hope that in time, diversification saves the day.

All these represent different beliefs about how financial markets operate. Whatever you do as an investor, such beliefs underpin your line of reasoning. Are you aiming to gain exposure in a market? Then you're basically familiar with the Capital Asset Pricing Model (CAPM). Interested in index investing? In that case, you probably implicitly adopt the Efficient Market Hypothesis as your guiding principle. More interested in realizing excess returns? In that case you probably spit on the Efficient Market Hypothesis.

A secret, undiscovered world lies behind these apparently innocent remarks by trustees, and it pays to know about it. It forms the DNA of investment management, and just as with DNA, there is a huge variation out there. Chapters 5 to 14 indulge you in uncovering these underlying assumptions. But the first step is to take a harder look at investments and why there's a huge variation. We will see we are not dealing with a normal field of science, and realizing this has some major consequences: pragmatic beliefs rather than hard theories guide us in our investment decisions.

3.2   Investing: Art or science?

Investing theory and practice have developed dramatically over the past five decades, yet there still is no objective framework around as to how we view capital markets and how to apply these insights for investment purposes (Lo 2005). In the 1950s, the investment philosophy boiled down to a simple approach: stock selection determined which securities were included in the portfolio, beginning with a careful analysis of a company's income statement and balance sheet. To founding fathers Graham and Dodd (Graham and Dodd 1951), developing financial ratios from the accounting record of companies was a key element for investment decisions.

A paradigm shift took place from the 1960s onwards with the work of Harry Markowitz (Markowitz 1970), which focused on assembling stocks into portfolios to minimize risk at an acceptable level of return: the "don't put all your eggs in one basket" principle. His main conclusion: portfolio construction is more important than picking individual stocks or timing markets.

The 1970s marked the concept of systematic risk. Active management – earning excess returns relative to benchmarks – met its counterpart in the 1980s with passive management – cleverly combining exposure to different markets to give investors the systematic risk and return they needed. In the 1990s, new investment strategies were developed at an astronomical pace, based on derivatives markets that were just 25 years in existence. Views then evolved further; active management since the turn of the century has increasingly meant earning absolute returns, leaving benchmarks out of the equation, with investment managers proclaiming they have forged a felicitous union between exploiting inefficiencies in the financial markets (active management), and clever financial engineering to achieve the right degree of systematic risk. All are different views of capital markets that still co-exist, sometimes in harmony and sometimes at odds with one another.

Yet none can be pinpointed as the right one. Theories in investments and finance simply do not have the same degree of confidence as theories in physical sciences for three reasons (Raymond 2008). First, finance is a relatively young discipline. Modern finance is roughly 50 years old, while other disciplines have been shaped over several hundreds of years. The main theories have not been road tested; basic premises are not conclusive. For example, for more than 30 years economists have hotly debated whether financial market pricing is efficient or not.

Such a debate has far-reaching consequences. Those who believe that markets are efficient advocate indexing and other passive strategies such as buy-and-hold, weathering the peaks and troughs of price cycles. Believers in inefficient markets usually invest in what they perceive as undervalued stocks, sectors or assets, and do not shy away from market-timing investment (Brav and Heaton 2001). In addition, the seemingly new regime with lower investment returns and ageing populations will severely test the extrapolative power of theories. Additionally, financial data is very "noisy".

It requires a lot of effort to extract relevant information from price signals, and the predictive power of models for future returns is generally low. New mathematical techniques, the field of econometrics, were developed to cope with this, but only succeed to a limited extent.

In other words, investment management is not a hard science like physics or chemistry; it is above all a social science. A truly scientific investment theory would be based on an equation derived from proven laws of nature that specify how we get from point A to point B in the future (Sherden 1998). Based on these laws, we have a pretty clear idea of when the tide turns, when the Haley comet visits our earth, and when the tide turns on the Spanish coast. We can accurately predict how long it takes a car to come to a complete standstill after hitting the brakes at 120 kilometers per hour. Models are based on characteristics such as mass, gravity, velocity, that can be clearly defined and precisely measured, and this enables precise predictions to be made (Gray 1997). Scientific theories and forecasts for economies and financial markets are impossible for this very reason: there are no proven natural laws underlying the behavior of social systems. Economists therefore opt for a second-best approach, constructing yardsticks like utility or risk tolerance to *emulate* hard science. Analysts might make predictions based on theories, but such theories are not laws of nature and do not stand the test of scientific methods. Their models have limited applicability because the yardsticks are inherently unstable as well as difficult to establish objectively: risk tolerance varies immensely per person, or before and after a financial crisis.

The second factor setting investment management and economics apart from the hard sciences is that while for example physics can test hypotheses through controlled experiments, this is very difficult in the case of economics and investments (Gray 1997). Economists are creative in circumventing this restriction by gathering as much data as possible and looking for common denominators (when equities go up, *on average*, bonds do not increase as much in value).

Alternatively, we focus on the actor who sets it all in motion – hence the surge in the study of behavioral finance. While general theories are nearly impossible to construct, modeling structural regularities and irregularities in human behavior is a promising avenue, since human behavior has a tendency to endure for longer periods. However, this allows partial insights at best. With human behavior, we have a pretty clear picture of why markets overreact. This brings us nowhere near the answer to the question of how much or for how long stock markets overreact, insights investment managers are craving.

The bottom line remains: we still cannot conduct experiments in a controlled environment and draw general conclusions. At best, these general theories result in forecasts that are little more reliable than simple naïve guesses (Sherden 1998). This sobering view resonates in a wide range of debates in investment management, as Part II will show. That is why so many debates never really reach a firm conclusion and keep haunting investors and trustees: proponents of active management – with the ultimate aim of earning more than a benchmark – have just as much ammunition in the form of anecdotal evidence or research to prove their case to sympathizers of passive management as the other way round – especially when active management does not pay off. There is no single objective truth in the financial markets, just an accumulation of learning by doing and adapting to new realities.

Gray (1997) raises another point: certain humans have the capacity to influence the course of economics and finance in fundamental ways. *Policy-makers* have shaped economic growth, inflation and, as side-effect, competitiveness through monetary policy, while on a micro level ambitious investment managers have the capability to arbitrage away any inefficiency that exists. As we progress, our knowledge accumulates, changing the design of the models. The positive consequence is that investors and policy-makers take an adaptive approach to events. For example, regulators and governments acted swiftly when the severity of the credit crisis in 2008 became clear. One can debate the effectiveness of the measures, but decision-makers had definitely learned lessons from previous crises: the need for swift and decisive action was one of them.

When investors influence the course of finance and investment, this also implies that we cannot simply take for granted that occurrences from the past will re-occur in the future. Every generation has a different mental framework about macro-economic policy-making and investor attitudes, and has accumulated knowledge from earlier events, which makes it risky (maybe even irrational) to assume that history repeats itself.

We can point to a positive equity return between 1900 and 2008 in the US and use this to justify the idea that equities are a sweet deal in the long term, but this amounts to combining different periods where financial markets have adapted themselves to changing regulation and economic conditions, and assuming that this provides some indication for the future. That's a leap of faith. Analysts and researchers are now embroiled in a debate about whether investment results since the 1990s are indicative for long-term equity returns, let alone whether the investment results achieved in the 1920s are indicative. Evolving and adapting financial markets imply that results from the past provide valuable information, but also emphasize the need to develop our own views on the future to embed future adaptation.

3.3   The basics of an investment belief

The message of the previous section is clear: better investment management is not necessarily achieved simply by building better models. During the recent credit crisis, critics have pointed to the failing econometrics models used by investment managers for risk management and actuaries for pension fund asset liability management. But improved models would not have helped managers – help begins with a better understanding of the financial markets, their underlying dynamics and how investors view them.

Investment beliefs accept the reality that economics and finance cannot be captured in hard, predictive models. Instead, they encompass a *view* on how (other) market participants learn or fail to learn on the capital market. Consider the case for active management, where investors basically value a security by discounting the future cash flows of a security and comparing this to the current price (Minahan, 2006). The trading strategy is straightforward: buy if the value is higher than the price, and sell if the value is lower than the price. In real life, failure to do so successfully in active management is well documented. Human judgment and human behavior stand in the way of an objective valuation and trading strategy. One does not know the future cash flows of the security, nor is there agreement about the discount rate to be applied. To make matters worse, if the security is an illiquid asset, determining the current price itself is the result of an arbitrary valuation. Alongside the failure to achieve an objective assessment, the effect of dissemination of news about the security also creates further noise when investors hold different views, as extensively documented by behavioral finance.

The question here is not *why* the market is unable to deliver a consensus on the future cash flows or the discount rate. Rather, the real question is whether an investment manager has a clear view on what the (mis)pricing of securities and assets is, and *how* the manager is able to identify these mispricings and exploit them. This is the basis for a workable investment belief. We therefore argue that an investment belief system or philosophy has four main elements: basic beliefs, beliefs in relation to theory, beliefs in relation to strategy and beliefs in relation to organization, as depicted in Figure 3.1.

Basic investment beliefs are generally formulated as observations of a mechanism of human behavior in the financial marketplace, such as

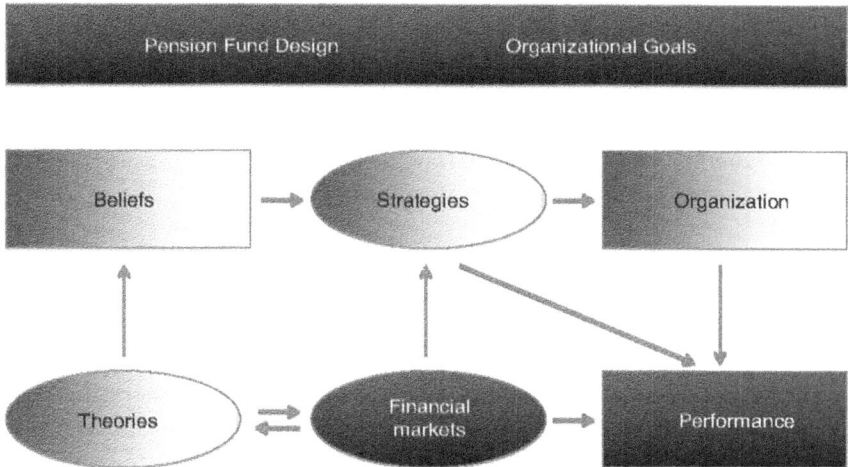

Figure 3.1 Framework for analyzing investment beliefs

"markets overreact". Since beliefs generally deal with the fallibility of human behaviour, they tend to contain an element of judgment. It is this judgment that implicitly enables the asset management organization to use such behaviour in a more sophisticated way. The term "belief" accepts that there are no objective truths in the financial markets, and that investors can choose to interpret observations or mechanisms differently.

Investment theory argues about whether there is a sound basis for the investment belief. What is it about the mechanism that causes the mispricing? More important, is it a structural phenomenon that is repeatable in the (near) future? Can we identify beforehand performance measures that are directly linked to this investment belief; in other words, can we verify the claim that is made here? If a mechanism is observed in the financial markets but arguments for a theoretical basis cannot be found, then the investment organization runs the risk of not knowing how to design a strategy around this if it cannot predict future performance.

The **investment strategy** describes how the investment belief can be exploited. An investment strategy is nothing more than a plan or approach, deciding on four issues: 1) the investment rules, 2) the quantitative and qualitative parameters to be used with the investment rules, 3) the investment instruments that can be used, and 4) the time horizon that applies to the rules. Investment rules can be straightforward and are usually formulated in an "if..., then..." syntax: *if* an asset class seems undervalued, *then* over-weight the asset in the portfolio. The question here is: what determines undervaluation? For example, continuing our market overreaction example, an exploitable strategy is to sell stocks the same day after a positive news announcement and buy them the same day after a negative one, and close the positions two weeks later when the overreaction effect subsides. To decide whether the investment strategy is worth following up on, the following issues are also tackled in this phase:

- Is it the most effective way to allocate the risk budget? And as we consider in Chapter 10 on risk management beliefs – is it the most effective way to allocate the risk budget in different – more extreme – risk regimes?
- Is the investment strategy effective; does it help realize the objectives of the organization? Deciding on the scale and scope of the strategy involves a delicate balance that is more than just mechanically optimizing the portfolio. To start with, the scale and scope of the strategy must be sufficient to make it possible at the evaluation phase to distinguish its impact from noise in financial markets. Scaling up the strategy has its limitations though. For managers with diversified portfolios, the impact of the strategy is restricted at some level. The risk manager will point out the potential concentration risk; the performance of the total portfolio should not be unduly affected by one strategy alone. The investment manager worries about the relative market size, and avoiding being "cornered" in specialized markets. This is illustrated in Figure 3.2.

Finally, the **organization** addresses the issues that an organization has to take care of to exploit the investment strategy successfully. Ideally, the investment process links the exploitation of the investment belief to performance measures that relate directly back to the investment belief. An organization has to be set up to implement the strategy, whether this is internal management of assets or selection and monitoring of external managers. At the same time, governance has to be set up. What is needed is the combination of the right incentives for the portfolio managers to perform, a clear delineation of responsibilities between investment managers and trustees as shaped by the investment mandate, and a supervisory function that monitors, understands and also can intervene in the implementation once underway.

The interpretation of this approach is straightforward as shown in Figure 3.3. Consider once again the example of the overreaction belief. Standard finance theory – enshrined in the efficient market hypothesis – tells us that all (relevant) information is priced in the security. So what happens if oil company Royal Dutch Shell publishes a trading update, for

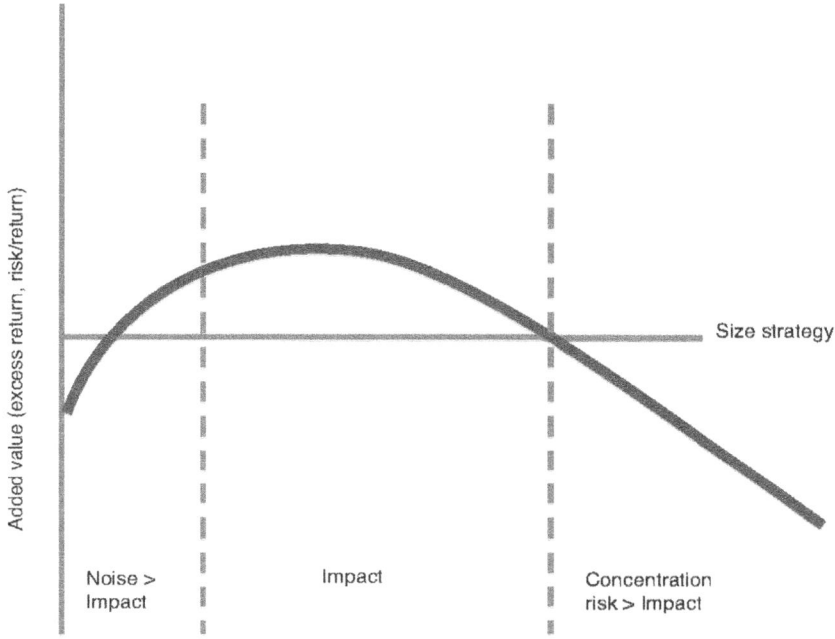

Figure 3.2 Trade-offs with an investment strategy

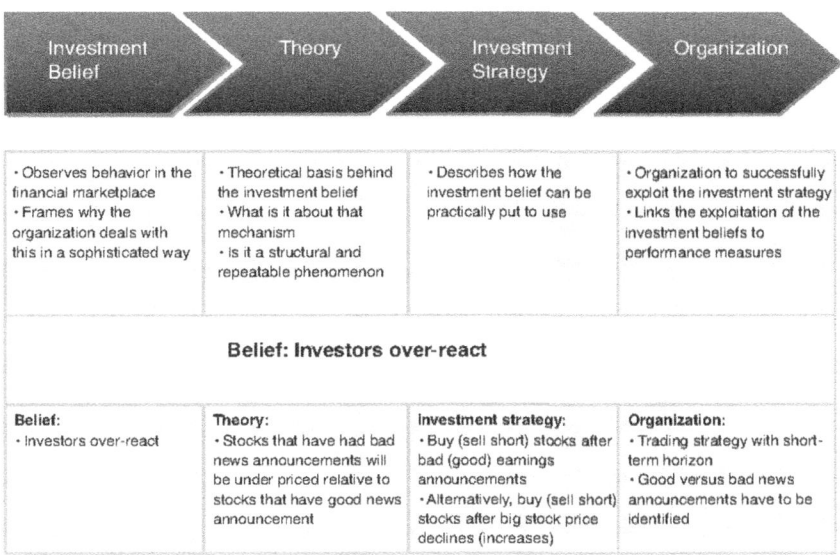

Figure 3.3 Investment beliefs in practice

example announcing that margins have improved despite falling demand for oil? Theory predicts an instantaneous shift in the price of a security. This however assumes that all investors receive the trading update, in a split second decide how it might affect the future valuation of the security, and then either buy or sell the security. The line in Figure 3.4A shows the valuation of the security over time. At t=1 the trading update is published. In reality, this is a rather overoptimistic view on how investors process information. Perhaps it is more realistic to consider that information trickles down to investors. This trickling down might be with a twist – investors first react to Shell's trading update with their gut feelings, and only later take the time to assess the information more thoroughly. This over- and under-reaction effect, as shown in Figure 3.4 has been documented by several authors (cf. De Bondt and Thaler 1985; Dreman and Berry 1995). Additionally, overconfidence can also arise when investors overestimate the precision of the information (cf. Tversky and Kahneman 1974; Shefrin and Statman 1994).

So we have a view of the financial markets here that can be distilled into an investment belief – investors overreact: it makes theoretical sense, and there is empirical evidence. Moreover, it might well be a robust investment belief. One of the appealing things about exploiting behavioral biases is that human behavior changes very slowly, if at all. Strategies that exploit human behavior and have generated positive returns in the past are likely to continue to be successful in the future (Fuller 1998).

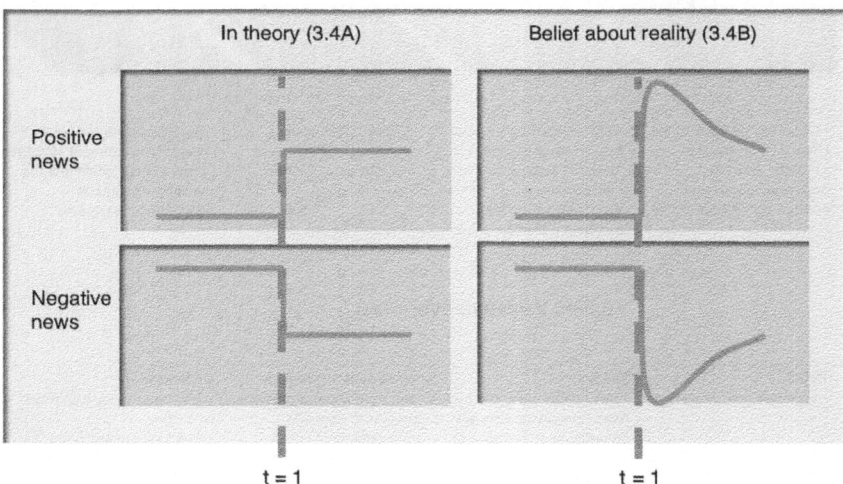

Figure 3.4   The basis for the overreaction belief

If all of the four boxes (belief, theory, strategy, organization) can be ticked then there is a workable investment belief system in place. If one of the boxes cannot be determined or implemented, the investment belief might be flawed. Implementing a strategy based on a belief, but without a clear argument as to why, is like betting on the lottery. It's the equivalent of watching a trader making lots of money in the dealing room and the trader remarking that it is just gut feeling at work. The question of whether his success can be repeated in the future remains unresolved; chances are that it won't be.[1] Alternatively, not thinking through the organizational aspects also has its drawbacks. For example, Shell Pension Funds argues that if you neglect to minimize implementation costs, it becomes very hard to outperform through classic stock picking (Bartlema 2005).

The investment belief itself is not a reflection of consensus; it stands out as a belief against other beliefs. Another belief might well be that there is no overreaction, or if it exists, that it is extremely hard to exploit. This belief in turn leads to different conclusions regarding the investment strategies for the portfolio. That the relationship between risk and return in general shows an upward slope is no surprise to market participants; however, the view that there are unique risk/return opportunities that only pension funds can exploit lends itself to becoming a workable belief.

Translating the investment belief into a workable investment strategy and supporting organizations is crucial too. Empirical research from Inalytics, a consultant firm, shows that while active managers might have skill, they often fail to translate this into superior performance due to poor selling decisions. In a study, Inalytics found that the stocks sold impacted performance negatively by 0.94% per year. In other words, a good investment strategy leads nowhere if the implementation is flawed.[2]

3.4   Investment philosophy

We define investment philosophy as the *collection* of investment beliefs that the asset management organization considers its added-value in investment management. There's no prescribed number of investment beliefs; the number varies with the scale and reach of the investment manager. When you're an investment manager specializing in value strategies, the collection amounts to a few investment beliefs – you target a specific investment style and market, which is your backbone. Dutch civil servants' pension fund ABP on the other hand, investing 208 billion in almost every financial market worldwide,[3] holds ten different investment beliefs on which its investment organization is founded.

Table 3.1   Stylized investment beliefs (partly based on ABP Investments Strategic investment plan ABP 2007–2009)[4]

Stylized Investment Beliefs

---

1. **Investment risk is rewarded.** The fund's investment horizon, combined with the fact that outflows are required for a long period, means that the fund is well positioned to capture risk premiums.
2. **Diversification is a "free lunch".** Spreading of assets over different investment categories, styles, regions, etc. is the simplest way of improving the return vs. risk ratio.
3. **Alpha generates a positive contribution to the return.** Beating the market due to an active investment management approach, yields a positive contribution to the return on the portfolio.
4. **There is a premium for illiquidity.** Investors demand an extra premium for illiquidity in the form of an additional return. As a long-term investor, the fund is in a position to earn this premium.
5. **Innovation pays off.** By investing early in new developments, relatively high returns can be earned before a new investment opportunity is discovered by the general investment public and the extra return diminishes.
6. **Investing for the long term pays off.** The fund draws advantage from its ability to adopt an attitude of patience, earning risk premiums as well as improving return/risk ratio's that short-term investors cannot.
7. **Environmental care, social responsibility and corporate governance are important.** By embedding non-financial factors in the investment process the risk vs. return profile can be improved.

The larger and more diversified the investment management operations, the more debates the fund tends to encounter in formulating investment beliefs (Table 3.1).

The other way around can be somewhat of a warning signal – large, diversified managers with only a few investment beliefs or small managers with an extensive set of investment beliefs might easily suffer as a result.

An investment philosophy as a collection of investment beliefs sounds rather straightforward, but the investment organization should keep an eye on two essential elements: are the investment beliefs a *dynamic* set, and how do they *interact*? An investment philosophy is a *dynamic* set of core investment beliefs; Damodaran (2007) argues that you can go back to these investment beliefs to generate new investment strategies when old ones do not work. To determine that they do not work, you have to make them explicit and measurable. To generate new ones, you have to learn from the mistakes. The very concept of investment beliefs implies that mistakes will be made – it is after all a belief, and you are bound to pick one or two wrong ones every now and then. Most investors do a great job telling you how well they've done with their investment strategies. These are probably also the investors that led you to ride the waves of all the major hypes, not the organizations that do post-mortems and think about how to improve their investment philosophy.

Ideally, an investment philosophy combines multiple investment beliefs that provide the best fit for the client, given essential characteristics such as risk aversion, time horizon, and asset size. Multiple investment beliefs do potentially create alignment issues in the investment organization. Consider a pension fund that believes in long-term mean reversion (see below) and creates value versus growth portfolios. When the pension fund also believes in short-term active management and implements a (short-term) overreaction strategy, conflicts can arise. Based on the belief that securities revert back to a long-term average valuation or return (*mean reversion*), a security would be bought, whereas the strategy based on overreaction would mean selling the security. This is bewildering to trustees – the net position of equities has not changed, but the fund has to pay for the transaction costs anyway. In other words, trustees have to be aware of the relationship between the investment beliefs and resulting strategies – when investment beliefs are implemented in the design of the investment strategy and organization, which ones enhance each other, and which do just the opposite? Roberts (2004) introduces three types of relationships: *complementary*, *non-convex* and *non-concave*. Complementarity gives rise to clear patterns of coherence in investment beliefs. Non-convexity and non-concavity mean that there are several investment beliefs that are quite distinct. These relationships are illustrated in Figure 3.5.

Investment beliefs are *complementary* if putting into practice (more of) one investment belief increases the effectiveness of and returns from implementing the others. Developing a clear philosophy about the focus and impact of investment decisions (giving rise to alpha versus beta, core-satellite etc.) is enhanced if the organization also develops clear beliefs about the time horizon and costs. The American mutual fund investor Vanguard has developed strongly complementary beliefs, by stating that costs erode returns: "Keeping investment costs low, whether they are management fees or transaction costs, provides a major head start toward success. Cost is a predictable factor that investors can control – unlike financial market returns and volatility."[5] This belief really becomes powerful when combined with another belief of Vanguard, that "a long-term outlook matters. An approach based on short-term goals or tactics doesn't represent an investment philosophy. The risk of short-term price declines is too significant in the

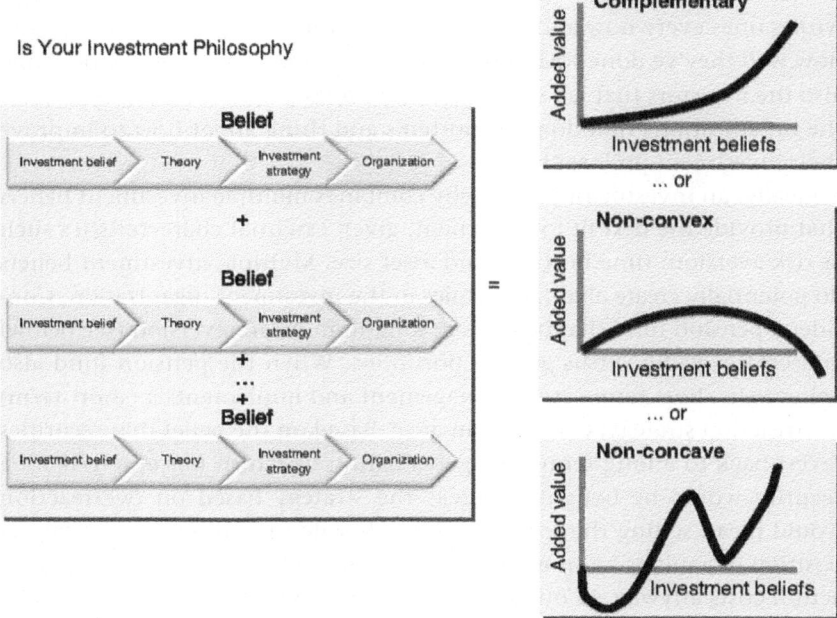

Figure 3.5   Relationships between investment beliefs

bond and stock markets to hazard money kept for short-term goals. Investing in the bond or stock market is for money that will be needed years from now."[6] The compounded interest effect of lower costs over a longer period is a real value driver for Vanguard's clients.

Non-convex means that if the consequent investment strategy of an investment belief is embedded, the successive increments of the investment strategy will decrease and perhaps become negative. There might in theory be a single best way (optimum) to implement the belief, but the best way in practice is to implement small changes and determine whether performance is increasing or from some point onwards, decreasing. Scaling alpha strategies or diversification fall into this category. Alpha strategies are all about earning excess returns by exploiting inefficiencies in the financial markets. Suppose a pension fund is smitten by the idea and allocates 50% of its assets to alpha strategies, and allocates this among 30 external investment managers. The fund's assumption: the end result should be a portfolio with a stable return, due to the collection of independent strategies. The end result might well be the opposite: an unwanted exposure to the financial markets, resembling the market risk that the pension fund was trying to steer away from in the first place.

Non-concavity presents another problem: there might be several approaches to an investment strategy, but the investment manager is unaware of them, and might end up implementing a suboptimal one. When a pension fund decides to invest in private equity, real estate or infrastructure, the underlying investment belief is that exploiting illiquidity premiums – getting a reward for investing in an illiquid market for a longer period – seems a good idea (see Chapter 6). Investing in private equity is however a large scale business, and there might be a high entry hurdle for initial investments. Once a fund has surmounted this, opportunities to grow further within the asset class are limited. In recent years, private equity managers have shown a tendency to increase the scale of their investments dramatically, going into large buy-outs. On the funding side, this requires large investors, so medium and smaller funds are squeezed out, and can only participate in small venture capital.

3.5   Embedding investment beliefs in governance

The chances of success in developing and implementing a coherent set of investment beliefs are only credible if this is embedded within the broader governance of the pension fund. After all, the investment beliefs system covers four areas (belief-theory-strategy-organization), and success depends largely on whether the organization is able to fit the puzzle together effectively and efficiently – but this is also just a part of the total governance design. Governance is one of those terms everyone knows until they are asked to reduce it to a few simple sentences. So a definition seems a good place to begin. According to dictionary definitions, governance deals with ideas and concepts around the exercise of authority or control. Who is in charge of what part of the investment process, what exactly do they need to be in order to be in charge, and how is the whole chain managed? We must look for insight into the act of exercising this authority, the underlying process for that exercise and the authority or powers that enable its exercise.

- You need to be clear on the goals that have to be achieved, and the risks that the organization has to take to achieve these goals.
- The executive board has to put the right incentives in place in order to be able to translate its long-term goals into strategic goals.

The basic goal of pension fund governance is to minimize the potential agency problems which can arise between the fund members and those responsible for the fund's management, and which can adversely affect the security of pension savings and promises (Stewart and Yermo 2008). Good governance goes beyond this basic goal and aims at delivering high pension fund performance while keeping costs low for all stakeholders. Good governance can have many positive side effects such as creating trust amongst all stakeholders, reducing the need for prescriptive regulation, and facilitating supervision.

In a study of a sample of large pension funds from six different countries dispersed across North America, Europe and Asia-Pacific, Clark and Urwin (2007) also conclude that superior performance is linked to strong governance. Their study identified various areas where the funds analyzed excelled, such as clarity of mission and effective risk management and performance monitoring. The report includes both governance capacity as well as investment strategy in the risk profile of the fund, and recommends linking the investment strategy of the fund to the governance capability of the board. For example, boards should first decide whether they are capable of monitoring alternative investments effectively before debating whether to include such instruments in their investment strategy.

The absence of governance and good decision-making can create substantial opportunity costs. For example, lagging results prompted an external review of the Kentucky Retirement Systems. The investment performance of the $17 billion Kentucky Retirement System and $15.6 billion Kentucky Teachers Retirement System had been significantly underperforming similar systems across the country, according to a report on a study conducted for Governor Steve Beshear's public pension working group. Kentucky Retirement had an opportunity cost of $1.5 billion (8% of assets) for the ten years ended June 30 2008 and Kentucky Teachers, $3.5 billion (22% of assets). Failing governance and a lack of insight into developments in investment policies were considered to be the main factors (Kentucky Public Pension Working Group 2008).

Kentucky Retirement Systems is but one example of what Keith Ambachtsheer dubs the "governance gap". A governance gap arises when governance characteristics of a fund differ from a best practice peer group. For publicly quoted companies, the relationship between governance and market value is increasingly being recognized (cf. Aggarwal et al. 2007). Similarly, the central role played in investment management by the governing board in ensuring good governance and raising long-term investment value for all stakeholders is becoming a serious agenda item for managers and boards.

For example, Ambachtsheer et al. (2006) show how good governance and good performance are linked. Surveying pension funds based in Australia, New Zealand, Canada, the United States and Europe, their analysis takes pension fund executives' own opinions of how well their governance is working as a proxy for good governance, with pension fund returns over a passive asset benchmark taken as a performance proxy. They conclude that the "poor-good" governance gap as assessed by pension fund CEOs (or equivalents) themselves has been worth as much as 1–2% of additional return per year – and the authors think this is probably an underestimate.

In a later article, Ambachtsheer et al. (2007) identify the main governance weaknesses as poor selection processes for members of the governing board, a lack of self-evaluation of board effectiveness, and weak oversight by the board. Other specific problems include lack of delegation clarity between board and management responsibilities, board micro-management, and non-competitive compensation policies in pension funds. Clark and Urwin (2008) develop this theme further and distill an advance from gap analysis to best practice recommendations for well-governed funds, which we will discuss more extensively in Part III, "Embedding Beliefs".

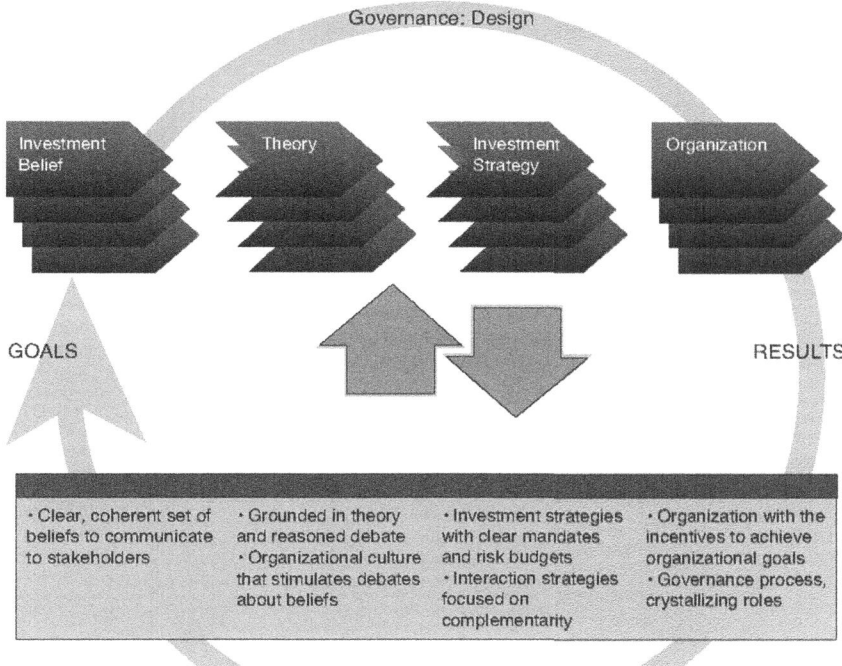

Figure 3.6   Investment beliefs in the governance process

Developing and implementing an investment beliefs system is an integral part of well-governed funds (Figure 3.6). As we argued in 3.3, an investment philosophy comprises multiple investment beliefs. In theory, each investment belief has its own theory, investment strategy and organization. The number of investment beliefs and the ability to bundle subsequent investment belief steps determine the quality of governance required to be set up and manage the investment process, and adapt it to changing environments. The challenge for investment organizations is to select and combine investment beliefs that reinforce each other – or at least are not in conflict with each other – and allow efficient investment strategies, as well as sharing of organizational processes for effective implementation.

3.6   Investment beliefs and performance

Which investment beliefs are crucial or irrelevant to success when investment beliefs are linked to the performance of a pension fund? There is no straightforward answer to this question, since the answer depends on the combination of investment beliefs, how well thought out they are, and how effective they were implemented. But there is growing evidence of a direct relationship between the observed investment beliefs held by pension funds and performance. A study, encompassing 600 pension funds worldwide between 1992 and 2006 unearthed investigated the investment beliefs held by pension

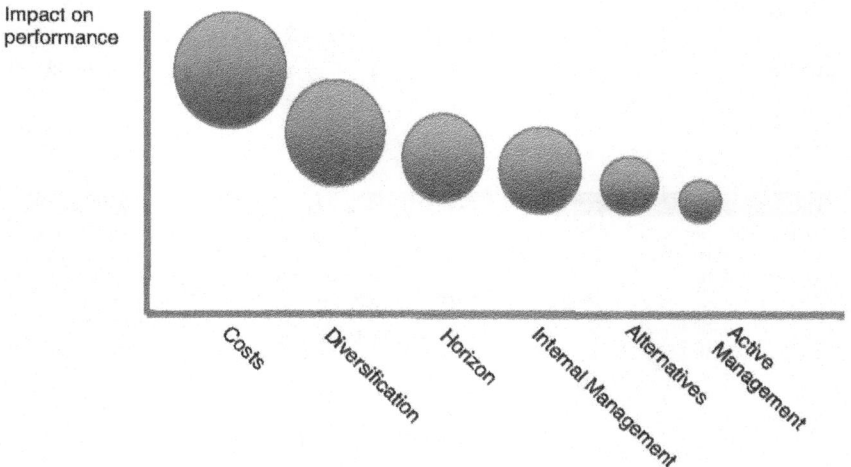

Figure 3.7   Impact of investment beliefs on performance (Koedijk et al. 2010)

funds by analyzing the realized investment strategies and deducing the investment beliefs behind them (Koedijk et al. 2010). Some investment beliefs are more important than others (Figure 3.7) to performance. Equally relevant is the finding that total performance depends on the combination of investment beliefs (the investment philosophy), where the implementation of certain beliefs are not *complementary*, and even *non-concave*, limiting the potential return-risk of the fund (see also section 3.4).

Other research results from the worldwide pension study indicate the following:

- Greater size allows funds to operate more cost effectively and take on more varied assets in order to diversify effectively. Larger funds have the resources to invest in innovative new strategies, thereby earning first-mover advantages, although their size causes some funds to increase their use of cost-intensive strategies (cf. Ambachtsheer 2009), thereby offsetting potential improvements in return-risk relationships.
- Pension funds do tend to earn excess returns with active management. Excess returns improve when funds increase their share of internal management, which lowers costs. However, a fund's return-risk trade-off does not necessarily improve with excess returns.
- Diversification is manifested in the return-risk trade-off. Greater portfolio diversification is associated with higher return-risk ratios. Diversification by adding more alternative strategies, however, apparently offsets the return-risk improvement.
- Due to their long-term horizon and the general absence of short-term liquidity constraints, pension funds are better able than other participants are to invest in illiquid and/or alternative investments, and they are better equipped to earn an illiquidity premium. Nonetheless, investing in these asset classes does not always improve the overall return-risk.
- Internal management cuts both ways: it effectively lowers costs and increases net returns. The second effect is probably more intangible; the management of internal mandates provides the knowledge needed to monitor external mandates effectively and to improve the principal–agent relationship.

If anything, these results are an example of the current state of research in investment governance: a link between investment beliefs and performance is there, but the recipe for implementation is not a straightforward one. Trade-offs, and interdependencies between investment beliefs have to carefully weighed for each fund.

3.7 A tour d'horizon

Part II will delve deeper into investment beliefs. There is no definitive set of investment beliefs, and our discussion will show that there are many unresolved debates that a trustee should be aware of. To determine the best practice, we have conducted a worldwide survey over the years, collecting investment beliefs from large as well as smaller pension funds. Table 4.1 presents the documented investment beliefs for both types of pension funds. Several authors (Ambachtsheer 2004, 2007; Slager and Koedijk 2007) have identified elements that can be addressed in an investment belief, providing the basis for the survey. When formulating investment beliefs, the asset manager has several stakeholders to consider, and needs to differentiate between what he can and what he cannot influence. Furthermore, he might also consider the relationships/interdependencies with non-capital markets.

Based on these considerations, we cluster investment beliefs into four sets. The first set addresses financial markets; the second set considers the added value of the investment process. We also identify a set of beliefs about the firm's own organizational skills, and finally one about sustainability and corporate governance. These four sets of investment belief are explicated in Figure 3.8.

An informed and soundly reasoned decision about the asset allocation and investment strategy begins with a view on financial markets: how does

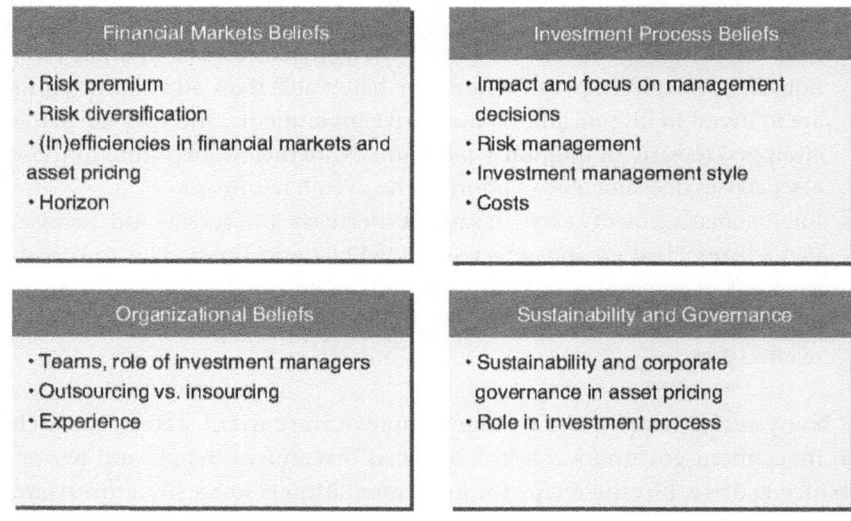

Figure 3.8 Investment beliefs

an investor view (structural) relationships between risk, return, and asset pricing? Roughly 28% of pension funds' investment beliefs – 25% for asset managers – deal with the risk premium, diversification, or the investment horizon. Pension funds however emphasize risk diversification (9%) while asset managers focus on (in)efficiencies in financial markets and their link to asset pricing (15%).

An investment process combines all the necessary steps to move from conceptualizing the investor's mission to realizing the returns in relation to the risk attitude and to previously set goals. The investment process emphasizes the different components that are needed for an investment strategy to be successful. 43% of the investment beliefs of pension funds deal with investment process related beliefs, the most important being the impact and focus of the management decisions, and the choice of investment management style. Less frequently quoted beliefs concern the choice between passive and active management, the focus on the cost of the investment process, and risk management.

How much thought (and research) has gone into the organizational setup and structure of the pension plan, and how it manages its own or external managers? This is addressed by the organizational beliefs, for example the belief about the role an investment manager should play in the organization to add value, or the choice between in- and outsourcing. Asset managers tend to emphasize the role of teams more than investment managers (16% compared to 6%), which can probably be explained by their commercial orientation, and makes intuitive sense given the fact that their teams are part of their commercial arsenal.

4
Why Pension Investors and Asset Managers Differ

Summary

✓ Asset managers are not pension funds and vice versa. Asset managers and pension funds each hold a different "basic kit" of investment beliefs.

✓ Asset managers use investment beliefs to demonstrate their competitive advantage, whereas pension funds use them as an effective tool for reasoned debate and decision-making.

✓ Pension funds also use their investment beliefs to mitigate potential information problems between trustees and investors.

Perhaps one of the puzzling aspects of the investment industry is that pension funds and asset managers seem to get along so well. In the past years, the costs and complexity of trustees' investments has been steadily rising. So have the incomes of asset managers, their advisors and other intermediaries, despite the fact that asset managers have not been able to fulfill expectations of investment returns. Pension funds and asset managers clearly do not share the same beliefs. Nor should they, as this would stifle innovation in products and services and progress in new investment concepts. In this chapter, we demonstrate these striking differences. But first, we look into why they are different – what economists refer to as the principal–agent problem.

4.1 It all makes sense

The asset manager provides a service, involving management of a portfolio on behalf of a client. Unless the asset manager is perfectly monitored by

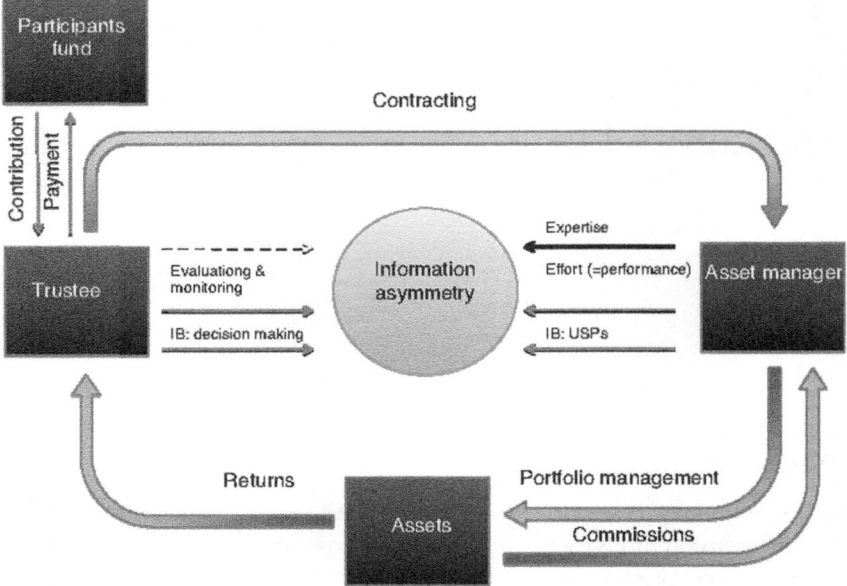

Figure 4.1   Principal–agent problem between trustee and asset manager

the pension fund and/or a foolproof contract is drawn up, the manager may act in his own best interests, generating excessive income for himself, contrary to the interests of the pension fund (Davis and Steil 2004). The information asymmetry between them gives rise to the so-called principal–agent problem, where the trustee can be considered as the principal hiring the asset manager as an agent (Figure 4.1).

Aspects of fund management can be seen as ways to reduce this principal–agent problem. Most pension funds offer short (three-year) mandates, with frequent performance evaluation. The pension fund also imposes restrictions on the manager by means of a contract, containing strict rules or outright prohibition of practices like soft dollar agreements, where brokerage commissions (i.e. direct costs for the pension fund) paid by the fund manager comprise more than brokerage alone, for example including research and other favors. Also, fees are related to the value of funds at year-end and/or performance-related fees to prevent churning – engaging in excessive trading.

There is however a trade-off. Performance evaluation over a short period contrasts sharply with the nature of liabilities of pension funds, whose maturity may extend to 25 years or longer. And while performance fees sound an apt approach, they are not however a panacea and might even create new principal–agent conflicts. Consider for example a manager who is paid at the end of the year based on a percentage of excess returns earned in the preceding 12 months. If the manager reports a substantial loss midway through the year, that will create a strong incentive to pursue extra, perhaps unwarranted, risks in the second half to pick up the slack (Picerno 1998).

Principal–agent problems usually do not even surface, or they are settled discreetly. In most cases, when the asset manager performs disappointingly, the mandate is terminated early. Now and then the general public catches a glimpse of these problems. One of the landmark cases which became visible to the public was when the Anglo-Dutch soap powder and personal care giant Unilever took Merrill Lynch Investment Management (then named Mercury Asset Management) to court in the UK in 2001. Unilever alleged that MLIM managed £1 billion of its pension assets negligently in 1997 and early 1998. During that period, the pension fund underperformed an agreed benchmark by 10.6%. Unilever claimed that the failure was largely caused by excessively risky investment decisions chiefly taken by Alistair Lennard, the manager responsible for the fund. Unilever's total fund is one of the country's largest, with 110,000 members and £4 billion of funds. MLIM denied negligence and claimed that unprecedented market conditions, including the unexpected rise of sterling against the German Deutschmark, were to blame for the poor performance of the fund.[1]

The Unilever–Merrill Lynch clash is a typical example of the principal–agent problem between trustees and external managers. But a principal–agent problem can also arise within the fund itself, when for example employees have difficulties in making the distinction between a pension fund and asset manager. This might result in the relatively harmless adoption of exciting new investment strategies. At the other extreme, fraud is the most visible outcome. In 2008, fraud cost the €13.4 billion Dutch pension fund of electronics company Philips an estimated €150 million. The fraud case revolves around the donation of real estate in exchange for bribes, as two pension fund directors allegedly were bribed to deal in Philips real estate for too high or too low a price. The difference between the transaction price and the real value then ended up in the pockets of others. Owning direct real estate turned out to be the smoking gun. The fund, fully aware of its principal–agent tensions, began restoring the balance by dismantling its real estate portfolio at the end of 2007, selling its real estate holdings to real estate investment funds.[2]

So how do the differences between asset managers and pension funds play out? The investment beliefs surveyed allow us to draw up a stylized

Table 4.1   Survey of published investment beliefs of asset managers and pension funds

| | | Organization type | | | |
| | | Pension fund | | Asset Manager | |
		Count	Column %	Count	Column %
Financial markets	Risk premium	10	6.4% ✓	2	2.5%
	Risk diversification	14	9.0% ✓	2	2.5%
	(In)efficiencies in financial markets/ asset pricing	9	5.8%	12	15.0% ✓
	Horizon	10	6.4%	4	5.0%
		43	27.6%	20	25.0%
Investment process beliefs	Impact, focus of management decisions	34	21.8% ✓	15	18.8%
	Risk management	6	3.8%	6	7.5% ✓
	Investment management style	25	16.0%	14	17.5%
	Costs	2	1.3%	1	1.3%
		67	42.9%	36	45.0%
Organizational beliefs	Teams, role of investment managers	9	5.8%	13	16.3% ✓
	Outsourcing vs. insourcing	5	3.2%	0	0.0% ✗
	Experience	1	0.6%	3	3.8% ✓
	Other	5	3.2%	3	3.8%
		20	12.8%	19	23.8%
Sustainability and corporate governance	Sustainability & corp. governance in asset pricing	4	2.6% ✓	0	0.0% ✗
	Role in investment process	5	3.2% ✓	1	1.3%
		9	5.8%	1	1.3%
Other beliefs	Pension liabilities	7	4.5% ✓	1	1.3%
	Goal	3	1.9%	1	1.3%
	Other	7	4.5%	2	2.5%
		17	10.9%	4	5.0%
	Total Count	156	100.0%	80	100.0%

picture of the differences between pension funds and asset managers. We developed a dataset of 40 pension funds and asset managers with publicly-reported investment beliefs.[3] Table 4.1 clearly shows the differences between pension funds' and asset managers' investment beliefs and highlights the most striking and significant ones.

We will describe the profile in more detail in this chapter, but just to highlight the main point of Table 4.1: Asset managers use investment beliefs to demonstrate their competitive advantage, while funds as principals formulate investment beliefs as an effective tool for decision-making, and for mitigating potential informational problems stemming from a principal–agent relationship between trustees and investors (Koedijk and Slager 2009). Of course, there are more nuances:

- What they share. Pension funds and asset managers express comparable beliefs on their investment processes. Pension funds tend to stress which decision has the greatest effect, where asset managers tend to emphasize the role of risk management as the basis for an investment style.
- What sets them apart. Asset managers also tend to emphasize their views on asset pricing, which makes sense, since views on asset pricing offer a basis for active management. Asset managers also tend to stress the importance of their organization's qualities, especially the value of investment teams. This suggests that asset managers use their investment beliefs to

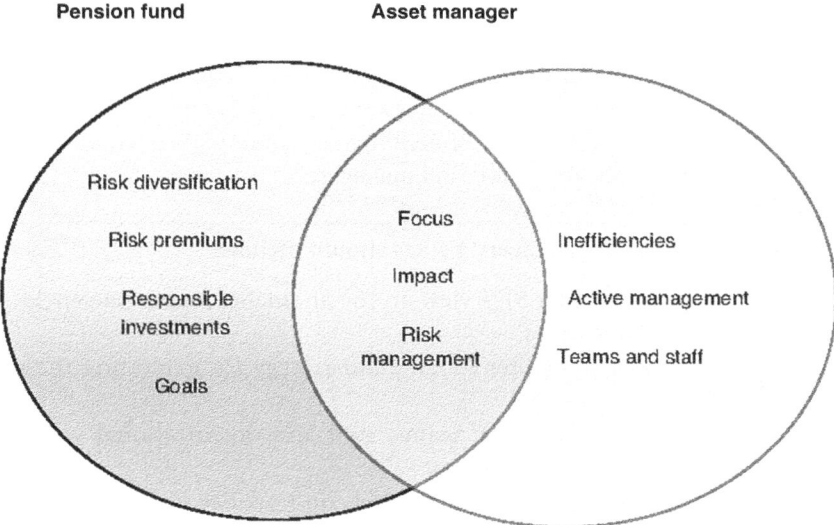

Figure 4.2   Beliefs shared and not shared by asset managers and pension funds

position themselves in the investment management market. Finally, some pension funds emphasize the role of sustainability factors in their investment philosophy and other beliefs that relate to organizational goals (see Chapter 14).

In the next sections, we delve deeper into the psyche of asset managers and pension funds, and describe a footprint based on their investment beliefs. Being aware of these differences makes sense and improves governance. Without being aware of them, pension funds might well align their own beliefs with the set of beliefs of asset managers (which they use like a marketing tool) when the funds select which asset manager they decide to employ. This lies at the root of many principal–agent problems between pension funds and asset managers.

4.2   The asset manager

Asset managers use investment beliefs to demonstrate their competitive advantage, providing a way to promote their added value to their prospective clients. It helps them to show that they are a trustworthy and effective agent. Asset managers sell performance. They are generally pretty confident that they can provide value for investors. They proclaim a "customer focused" approach, and re-label their product solutions to emphasize the partnering relationship that they aim for. Selling products is certainly not the main driver. Asset managers tend to over-emphasize the qualities of their organization. Asset managers, more than pension funds, also attach great value to the teams and staff of their investment organization, stressing risk management along the way. This suggests that asset managers use their investment beliefs to position themselves in the investment management market. Sustainability as a belief is practically absent for asset managers.

The basic kit of asset managers' beliefs should include:

- Inefficiencies (Chapter 5): a view on the anomalies and inefficiencies in the financial markets
- Investment style (Chapter 11): a plan/strategy for exploiting these anomalies
- Organization (Chapter 13): teams, staff and organizational values that make the investor stand out
- Risk management (Chapter 10): beliefs on how risk management is embedded in the organization

---

4.3   Pension fund

For pension funds, investment beliefs are an effective tool for framing, monitoring and evaluating decisions. A pension fund interprets the consequences of risk premiums in the financial markets, and emphasizes risk diversification. Both beliefs are consistent with a long-term view in investment management. Pension funds tend to stress which decision has the highest impact, while asset managers tend to stress the role of risk management as an argument for investment style. An asset manager also emphasizes his view on asset pricing, as it turns out that it is mostly inefficiencies that are the basis for active management. Finally, some pension funds emphasize the role of sustainability in their investment philosophy, along with other beliefs that relate to their organizational goals.

Overall, pension funds tend to be better investors than retail funds – or pick the better asset managers for that matter. Costs have a lot to do with this: Bauer and Frehen (2008) find that retail funds' costs are substantially higher than institutional funds' costs. Interestingly, their research also tries to explain the return differential. Costs only account for part of the difference; they argue that the remaining difference has to be found in agency costs – the fund is geared towards one goal only, providing a sound pension for its participants, and aligning investment beliefs, investment process and organization to achieve that goal creates more synergies than can readily be measured.

The basic kit of pension funds' beliefs should include:

- Risk diversification (Chapter 7): a view on which risks need to be diversified that are relevant to the fund
- Risk premiums (Chapter 6)
- Responsible investments (Chapter 14)
- Long term horizon (Chapter 8)
- Costs (Chapter 12)

Part II
Exploring Beliefs

Part II delves deeper into investment beliefs. What are their underlying assumptions? Are there intended and unintended consequences involved? There is no definitive set of investment beliefs, and our discussion will show that there are many unresolved debates that a trustee should be aware of.

We cluster investment beliefs into four sets. The first set addresses financial markets; the second set considers the added value of the investment process. We also identify a set of beliefs about the firm's own organizational skills, and finally one about sustainability and corporate governance. These four sets of investment belief are explicated in Figure 3.8.

An informed and soundly reasoned decision about the asset allocation and investment strategy begins with a view on financial markets: How does an investor view (structural) relationships between risk, return, and asset pricing? Roughly 28% of investment beliefs deal with the risk premium, diversification, or the investment horizon.

Investment process beliefs combine all the necessary steps to move from conceptualizing the investor's mission to realizing the returns in relation to the risk attitude and to previously set goals. The investment process emphasizes the different components that are needed for an investment strategy to be successful, the most important being the impact and focus of the management decisions, and the choice of investment management style.

How much thought (and research) has gone into the organizational set-up and structure of the pension plan, and how it manages its own or external managers? This is addressed by the organizational beliefs, for example the belief about the role an investment manager should play in the organization to add value, or the choice between in- and outsourcing.

Part II

Exploring E

5
Inefficiencies

Summary

✓ Market inefficiencies form the backbone of active management strategies to earn excess returns.

✓ It is relatively easy to identify inefficiencies. It is difficult enough to temporarily exploit inefficiencies successfully, but it is extremely difficult to find managers who can consistently exploit inefficiencies.

✓ There are two ways to turn inefficiencies into more return (alpha): either by generating or accessing new information or by processing existing information in a better way.

✓ Although asset managers are in favor of alpha strategies – they enable them to display their skills and earn nice fees – trustees should be cautious with them, as the evidence for consistent alpha returns is at best mixed and inconclusive.

5.1   Case study

General opinion has it that theory is boring for practitioners and exciting for academics. However, now and then theory galvanizes practitioners into hot debates. Warren Buffet, known for his outspoken opinions, declared that "I'd be a bum on the street with a tin cup if the markets were always efficient".[1] That is how Warren Buffet views the Efficient Market Hypothesis (EMH). Midway through 2009, Jeremy Grantham, a respected market strategist with institutional asset management company GMO, was also railing against the efficient market hypothesis,[2] and people paid attention.

Eugene Fama, a professor in the finance department of the University of Chicago started the ball rolling when he developed the EMH in the late

1960s. In short, it states that asset prices in security markets at any point in time "fully reflect" all available information on the market (Fama 1970). This matters to investors: if he is even partly right, then there is a lot of selling and buying in the securities market that does not make sense.

The logic of this theory is that "when information arises [on markets], this news spreads very quickly and is incorporated into the prices of securities without delay. Neither technical analysis, which is the study of past stock prices in an attempt to predict future prices, nor even fundamental analysis, which is the analysis of financial information such as company earnings and asset values to help investors select 'undervalued' stocks, would enable an investor to achieve returns greater than those that could be obtained by holding a randomly selected portfolio of individual stocks, at least not with comparable risk" (Malkiel 2003). Fama's shorthand translation: "I'd compare stock pickers to astrologers, but I don't want to bad-mouth the astrologers."[3]

Asset managers refuting the EMH look for mispriced securities, hoping to outperform the stock market with them. This is known as exploiting inefficiencies. One of the traditional inefficiencies-exploiting practices comes in the shape of a value investing strategy, a "classic" in the investment industry. The basic idea is to select securities that trade at a market price that is less than their intrinsic value, i.e. the value that one would expect the security to have according to fundamental analysis of company data and prospects.

LSV Asset Management, a quantitative US asset manager with a deep value-oriented investment style,[4] bases its investment philosophy on the premise that "superior long-term results can be achieved by systematically exploiting the judgmental biases and behavioral weaknesses that influence the decisions of many investors."[5] One should not be surprised that the three founders of LSV, all established finance professors at US universities,[6] have their roots in behavioral finance, the field that questions the validity of the EMH.

Believing in inefficiencies is one thing, but more important for your investments is exploiting these inefficiencies to "beat" the market on a regular basis. The $1 trillion[7] asset manager Vanguard knows this maybe like no other in the business. Specifically, Vanguard believes that "consistently outperforming the financial markets is extremely difficult."[8] This would be obvious from looking at the data: "Even the most professional investors fail to beat market indices over the long haul."[9] This means that Vanguard's investment activities are in line with efficient markets, or at least with markets that are efficient enough to make it extremely difficult

– if not impossible – to earn excess returns, especially after subtracting the management fees incurred for making them.

However, the debate is not completely black-and-white. Perhaps the majority of firms in the investment business adopt a position somewhere in the middle.

A very interesting example can be found in the views of US asset manager Dimensional Fund Advisors (DFA). As DFA's founders David Booth and Rex Sinquefield are former students of Eugene Fama it should not come as a surprise that DFA sticks really close to the belief that security markets are efficient. This results in the Santa Monica based asset manager using a passive approach of investing in predominantly small-cap stocks: a passive approach usually comes down to dull but solid index investing. However, Booth and Sinquefield do not rigorously follow an index; DFA's core belief is that "markets are efficient, but the firm adds value by not slavishly tracking the benchmarks."[10] Not sticking rigidly to an index gives them flexibility to keep out stocks that are not appealing according to DFA's criteria, and to keep stocks in that seem to be slightly undervalued. As DFA Mr. Booth likes to put it himself: "We're passive, but we're not stupid."[11]

5.2 Theory

An informed and soundly-reasoned decision about asset allocation and investment strategy begins with a view on financial markets: how does an investor view (structural) relationships between risk, return, and asset pricing? Beliefs about inefficiencies lie at the heart of crucial decisions investment committees make, as in the following investment styles:

Table 5.1 Investment styles

Strategy	Characteristics
Active vs. passive management	Adjusting portfolio to anticipate market and valuation changes (active management) to earn excess return or holding a portfolio, replicating the market index against low costs (passive management).
Alpha vs. beta management	Framework, separating market returns resulting from broad, diversified exposure to markets and strategies (beta), and attempts to add value (alpha) by combining strategies that exploit inefficiencies in the financial markets (Malkiel 2003).

Table 5.1 Investment styles – *continued*

Strategy	Characteristics
Value vs. growth investment style	Buying shares that appear underpriced according to fundamental – sector and company specific – measures (value) versus buying shares that might seem overpriced by fundamental measures but where this is attributed by investors to further growth prospects (growth).
Minimum variance portfolio	Investment strategy that minimizes risk rather than maximizing returns.[12]
Absolute return strategies	Strategies designed to earn absolute (positive) returns, rather than returns relative to a benchmark. Risk is simply the risk of loss (or of underperforming cash) rather than the risk of underperforming a benchmark. Investors can choose different approaches; one is the shorter-term trading style followed mainly by hedge funds, targeting relatively predictable, consistent and positive returns over the short term regardless of market conditions. The other takes a longer-term approach, targeting high absolute returns without reference to a benchmark, and accepting potentially higher interim volatility.[13]
130/30 strategies	Managers who combine a gross long position of 130% of the assets with a short position of 30%. The structure should give the managers more opportunity to generate alpha (see p. 34), exploiting inefficiencies on the short side as well as the long side (Engstrom et al. 2008). The strategy assumes an active management strategy, and is alluring to fund managers for the higher management fees. However, results so far have been disappointing, delivering lower returns than the benchmarks.[14]

Alpha, inefficiencies and active management are intertwined. In an attempt to unravel the knot, we start with a bit of theory, and then revisit the list above. Inefficiencies deal with a rather technical aspect of the financial markets; whether you believe they exist or not, they determine the bread and butter of a whole investment management industry.

Inefficiencies in financial markets deal with the question of whether the pricing of securities (and/or in aggregate the market or asset category) is perfectly efficient, or less than perfectly efficient. Efficient for investors does not mean "the price is right", but rather how fast investors adjust the price of a security to new information that is distributed. When the price of a security reacts almost immediately to new information, an individual investor is not able to earn an additional return with this information, so he cannot capitalize on it. The market is therefore said to be "efficient".

In the US, large corporations listed on the NYSE are traded in large volumes and covered by a large number of stock analysts, creating very efficient markets where returns are basically not predictable. For example, with more than 1,000 analysts tracking the ailing Citigroup stock, chances are that an individual analyst will be unable to infer more information about the stock's future prospects than the other 999. In other words, it does not pay to invest in information.

The value of information, however, increases when markets are less than perfectly efficient, but what then is the inefficiency, and how can it be exploited? Since the 1970s, investment professionals have adhered to either the strong variant of the efficient market hypothesis, or the semi-strong (or

Table 5.2   Illustration of efficiencies/inefficiencies investment beliefs

---

AXA Rosenberg – Investment Philosophy
AXA Rosenberg believes that "markets are reasonably efficient but not perfectly efficient..... We believe that it is extremely difficult to time markets or sectors consistently".[15]

Vanguard – Investment Philosophy – Belief #4
Vanguard finds that "consistently outperforming the financial markets is extremely difficult ... Identifying those investments that have outperformed in the past is simple. Identifying those that will consistently outperform in the future is extremely difficult. This task is particularly challenging in efficient markets".[16]

Pictet – Investment Philosophy – Investment Belief #2
Pictet holds a bottom up approach, believing that "the price of a financial asset should reflect the present value of its future cash flows".[17]

UBS Global Asset Management – Investment Philosophy
UBS finds that the "intrinsic value is determined by the fundamentals that drive a security's cash flow".[18]

---

even weak) efficient market hypothesis. Financial markets are not a homogeneous pool of capital however.

The return that can be earned with these inefficiencies is termed "alpha", and the way to earn it is either by generating or accessing better information (within legal limits of course), or by processing the information in a better way (Fuller 1998). Traditional investment managers try to generate a better information set by creating superior earnings forecasts or developing a deeper understanding of the economy or industry's profitability. These managers are known as traditional managers or fundamental managers.

Table 5.3   Illustration of exploiting inefficiencies

UBS Global Asset Management – Investment Philosophy
UBS believes that "discrepancies between market price and intrinsic value arise from market behavior and market structure providing opportunities to outperform."[19]

AXA Rosenberg – Investment Philosophy
AXA Rosenberg believes that "mispriced stocks can be identified by rigorous analysis of fundamental data."[20]

LAPP – Investment Policy
The asset mix decision is of critical importance to achieving Canadian's Local Authorities Pension Plan's objectives and will be the Board's major focus.[21]

Quantitative managers, on the other hand, assume that most information is commonly available to all investors and focus their energy on developing better procedures for processing this information to earn excess returns.

Alpha strategies are identified by their high tracking error to the benchmark – giving managers some leeway to develop an independent strategy – or even by the complete lack of a benchmark. Alpha drivers should result in a non-linear return pattern; their returns should not easily be mapped on the patterns of the total portfolio (Anson 2005). This suggests diversification advantages; portfolio managers tend to group alpha strategies together and present them as a separate asset class.

5.3   Debates to be aware of

However, trustees should be wary of alpha strategies. The evidence for alpha returns is mixed and inconclusive, and that's the good news. Consider the following facts:

- "You can't beat the market." An efficient financial market can be characterized as a zero-sum game in which the investors in aggregate can earn no more than the market return. In this situation, each investor's outperformance is exactly balanced by another investor's underperformance at the aggregate level. It is therefore extremely difficult to consistently outperform the market, especially when costs – such as management fees and transaction costs – are taken into consideration. In that case, an individual investor must outperform the market by at least the amount of his total costs to earn more than the market return. Academic research has investigated the probability of being able to consistently outperform the market through investment skills. There's compelling evidence that it is extremely difficult to maintain a positive track record over a longer period of time, when skill increasingly becomes a less influential factor.

- Alpha is a true hobby for asset managers, and not so much for pension funds, which makes sense. For trustees, it is just one potential source of returns they have to choose from, while for investment managers alpha is the true measure of their skill, increasing social standing (and personal income as well) in the investment management industry.
- One of the big mysteries in the investment industry is that institutional investors invest so much in active strategies, despite consistently disappointing results and research discouraging these strategies. It can probably be explained by a combination of two things. First, investing might well be one of the exciting things for trustees to do amidst their more serious administrative tasks, and they are not in a rush to make this duller. Second, trustees are human beings after all, and might simply dislike the idea that investment managers simply collect fees, and basically track indices. Let them sweat for their money!
- Alpha is time consuming and labor intensive; it seems a lot of work for a possible bit of extra return. The easy way out for pension funds is to persuade the actuary to increase the long-term target return in Asset Liability Management (ALM) by the expected alpha return, and simply embed it in the strategic asset allocation, abolishing alpha strategies along the way. The proponents of alpha will riposte by pointing out that one of the nice things about alpha is that it is not related to market movements in any way, so keeping it separate makes sense. Unfortunately, under extreme duress, even alpha has a tendency to dwindle away. In late 2007, PGGM, the Dutch pension fund for the healthcare sector, shifted a large chunk of its portfolio from active to passive management. The reallocation involved terminating the contracts of 15 external active managers running about €5 billion in assets and moving another €5 billion that was internally managed into its total beta portfolio. "In the classical alpha mandate (which seeks to outperform a benchmark), beta will often decline as alpha also declines under certain circumstances," said Marc Nuijten, head of alpha portfolios for PGGM. "You get hit twice ... Then it takes quite a long time to earn back the alpha." (Hua 2008).
- Alpha depends on skill in identifying and exploiting inefficiencies before everyone else does. The Greek philosopher Socrates may once have boasted that his knowledge consisted of knowing that he knew nothing. He would not have lasted in the financial services industry. Trustees will

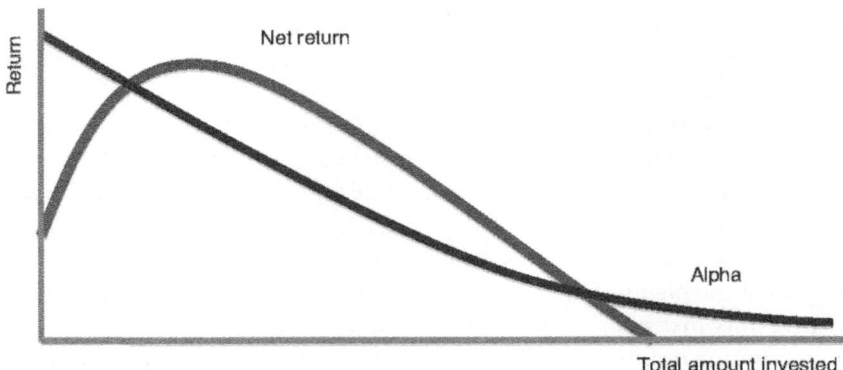

Figure 5.1   Investment manager's returns vs. asset under management growth

seldom encounter a portfolio manager boasting that he has no skill. Yet the empirical evidence is hugely disappointing, to say the least.

There is an inverted bath-tub shaped relationship between alpha and the amount of invested assets, illustrated in Figure 5.1. Even if trustees have been able to secure an investment manager with positive alpha, they should prepare for the worst. It is a safe bet that the alpha is temporary and in scarce supply. It starts out with the discovery of a market inefficiency, "providing a chance to scoop up money left on the table by the careless or the inept." (Warwick 2000). After an initial successful run, reducing the operating costs and perfecting the strategy, more assets directed toward the alpha strategy will simply dilute the potential earnings. And more managers pursuing a similar strategy will arbitrage the strategy away. This is basically the "Catch-22" in the industry. The investment manager's dream is to grow his business. The bigger the fund gets, the more revenue the managers generate, because they charge a fee that is (at least partly) based on the amount of assets under management. While the asset manager should have stopped investing at say $500 million – notably, the optimal amount of investment from the perspective of the pension fund manager, because the excess return is potentially highest – the asset manager basically keeps on earning more right up to $1,000 million. What this graph shows is that clients essentially never get the optimal result, and therefore have to work hard to align the asset managers' interests with their own. The natural alternative for pension funds would be to pay investment managers a percentage of the fund profits above the market benchmark (i.e. they are rewarded for alpha generation). Then the interests of the investment manager are more closely aligned with those of the pension fund investors and agency problems reduce. Many hedge funds do reward their managers in this way. However, this is flawed too. The asset manager still has an incentive to go for lower relative excess returns, as long as this is richly compensated by higher volumes of assets.

6
Risk Premiums

Summary

- ✓ Risk premiums represent the additional return investors require in return for the additional risk they take.
- ✓ However, the relationship between risk and risk premiums is non-linear and uncertain.
- ✓ Beliefs on risk premiums are embedded in investment decisions. Hence, small changes in assumptions may have significant consequences for portfolios and asset allocation.
- ✓ Assessing the future on historical risk premiums can be a dangerous business, because new investment strategies are based on historical data that may no longer fit the circumstances.

6.1 Case study

"Be like Yale!" Following up on the remarkably strong investment performance of Yale Endowment over the past 20 years, this slogan has become well-known among institutional investors worldwide. While few will publicly acknowledge that they are mimicking Yale Endowment Fund, asset allocation speaks louder than a thousand words. And why not be like Yale? After all, the Yale Endowment grew from $5.8 billion to $22.5 billion in the period from 1998 until June 2007, achieving annual net investment returns of 17.8%.[1] However, as Yale Endowment lost an estimated amount of 25%[2] of its value over 2008 and more and more investors are trying to invest like Yale does, the question arises as to whether the Yale model has just been a passing phase.

It all started when Nobel prizewinning economist James Tobin persuaded David Swensen to become the chief investment officer at the University of Yale in 1985. At that point in time, the Yale Endowment was worth just over $1 billion.[3] Swensen accepted the job and he began to build his vision on portfolio management based on insights that can be summed up in just a few important principles. For one, Swensen (2000) advocates diversification as it represents "a free lunch" that allows investors to reduce risk without sacrificing expected returns. But he also advocates an orientation toward equity, being well aware of the centuries-long time horizon that is relevant for the "permanent" endowments of universities.[4]

When Swensen started in 1985, nearly 80% of the Endowment was committed to US stocks, bonds and cash, an allocation which was, according to Swensen, far from desirable as this allocation did not exploit Yale's long-term horizon.[5] In subsequent years Swensen reallocated a large part of the Yale Endowment to nontraditional asset classes like "real assets", formed by real estate, oil and gas, and timberland (29.0%) and private equity (21.0%).[6] Swensen's approach worked: the Endowment grew in 20 years from just over $1 billion to more than $22 billion in 2008.[7]

The allocation towards nontraditional asset classes suits the emphasis on diversification and equity orientation well, as nontraditional equity classes are less correlated to conventional asset markets. The long-term horizon is well suited to exploit illiquidity premiums from these less efficiently priced markets via active management. So, the trick to "be like Yale" and record tremendous performances would be to put at least a substantial part of your eggs in the alternative investments basket. The number of universities and (institutional) investors that have expressed their attachment to the Yale model appears to be large and quite some copycats seem to be around.[8]

But being like Yale entails more than a hefty allocation to illiquid, alternative investments. As Swensen himself notes: "If you are going to invest in alternatives, you should be all in, and do it the way Yale does it – with 20 investment professionals who devote their careers to looking for investment opportunities."[9] The proviso that merely going into alternatives is not the solution is also addressed by Lerner in a study on university endowments: "The conclusion that more exposure to alternative assets will always lead to better performance is a false one." (Lerner et al. 2007). First, it is crucial to build up the skills to manage alternative investments – for the investment office as well as the overseeing board – as well as the network to source the interesting strategies way before the investment crowd is drawn to it. Experience and organization appear to be very important for successful investing in alternatives. Endowments like Yale typically have an outstanding, academic-oriented investment committee existing of alumni, who have often worked together for many years. Moreover, Ivy League endowments like Yale were among the first investors to get familiar with investing in alternatives. So to be sure, Yale has developed the skills which are necessary to be in alternatives.

Second, it is vitally important to "have a seat at the table". It is important to be close to some elite groups who are closest to new, innovative investment opportunities. As Yale has an enormous network of alumni, they have a major advantage in being the first to get acquainted with promising new opportunities. So from these perspectives the Swensen model is perfectly suited for Yale and exploits some sustainable advantages Yale has. But are they really sustainable?

Several studies[10] have shown that the alternative investment markets on which endowments like Yale have relied are particularly vulnerable to influxes of capital. The increased attention recently paid to those markets could lead to a deterioration in the factors driving Yale's high returns over the last decade and could make the model only temporarily suitable. Furthermore, markets change. Yale was (or still is) in a position to set the terms for its investments. However, the increasing power of venture-capital firms, who recognize the return potential and diversifying power they provide, could erode the bargaining power of institutional investors and increasingly lead to problems, even for large endowments like Yale.[11]

Add the 25% loss that the Yale endowment suffered over 2008 and it is no surprise that the wisdom of the Yale model has been called into question.[12] Meanwhile, Swensen replies to his critics by sticking to the principles of his model and his long investment horizon: "Yale built its portfolio on two basic principles: diversification makes sense and equity-oriented portfolios produce higher returns. Those are fundamental investment principles upon which you build a portfolio. They are not principles that go in and out of favor."[13] And, almost as an afterthought, he adds, "Critics are not thinking about what happened the ten years before and they are not giving us time to get through this crisis and see how it plays out for the Yale model against a more traditional portfolio."[14]

6.2   Theory

All investment managers deal with risk premiums, yet few formulate them explicitly. Standard asset pricing theory, most famously the capital asset pricing model (CAPM), predicts that investors expect a risk premium for bearing the systematic risk that they cannot diversify away. A positive

relationship between the expected return and variance of the market portfolio is intuitively appealing and has been called the "first fundamental law
of finance." (Ghysels et al. 2005)

Risk premiums are the additional long-term returns to be earned when
investors take on additional risk. The most famous one is the equity risk
premium: the additional return investors earn over long-term bond yields.
Risk premiums tend to be safely tucked away as assumptions in the appen-
dix of a long-term investment strategy study or asset-liability study. However, small changes in the premiums tend to have large consequences
for portfolio design. If you are upbeat on the prospects of equity, you are
expecting to earn a higher long-term equity premium. Yet investment risk
is contextual, and thus the riskiness of any investment depends in part
on the objectives of the investor. The relationship between risk and risk
premium is not linear. Also, the relationship for the investor is not linear.
In the current low return environments, institutional investors and the
regulators increasingly move towards an "S-Shape" interpretation of risk:
avoiding downside risk becomes more beneficial due to the increasing
penalties attached to it, such as covering the shortfall. The risk premium
plays an important role in the amount of risk an investor has to bear, and
takes different shapes (Figure 6.1). Beliefs about risk and risk-return relationships are based on the premise that investors are generally risk-averse

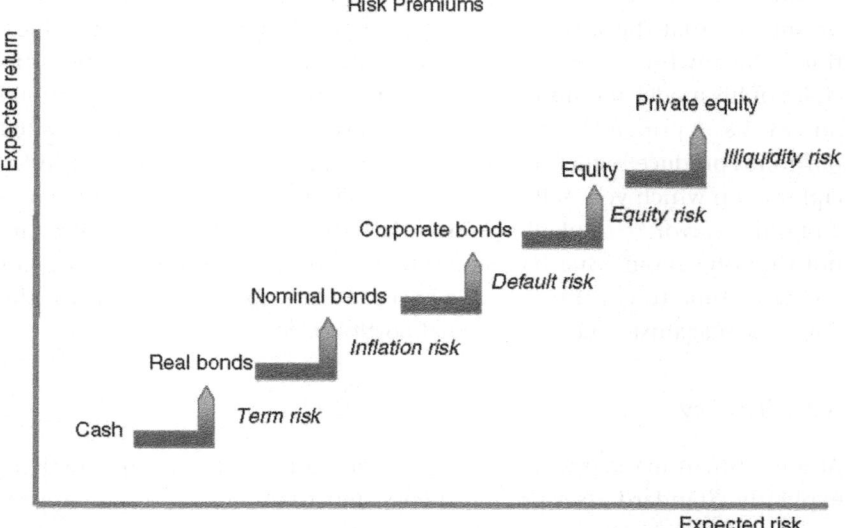

Figure 6.1   Risk premiums

and require expected risk premiums before they will hold investments they deem risky (cf. Ambachtsheer 2007). Five types of risk that are extremely relevant for premiums stand out: inflation risk, equity risk, default risk, longevity risk, and illiquidity risk.

6.2.1 Inflation risk

Inflation risk is a risk for pension funds whose liabilities are often linked to an inflation index, whether it be consumer prices or wages. In recent years, governments and companies have responded by issuing inflation linked bonds to cater for the demand for inflation hedging instruments, while asset managers and consultants have developed liability-driven investing services, taking into account that inflation risk is inherent in long-term liabilities.[15]

6.2.2 Default risk

In short, default risk – also known as credit risk – can be seen as the risk that you will not get paid. This happens when companies or individuals are not able to pay the contractual interest or principal on their debt obligations (in time). When a firm is in default, debt holders are given certain rights to the assets of the firm. Pension funds are typically more exposed to default risk as they invest in assets with a long duration to maturity, leaving more room for uncertainty. Measurement techniques for default risk are available. For example bond-rating companies Standard & Poor and Moody's apply these measures and rank bonds accordingly, based on their likelihood of default.

6.2.3 Equity risk premium

The equity risk premium is the long-term expected difference between the return on risky stocks and the return on safe bonds; over more than a century, investors in diversified US equities earned an average of 6% per year more than investors in US bonds (DeLong and Magin 2009). This gap shows why the equity risk premium is central to investments and to a large extent determines the substantial allocation of equities in portfolios. In academia, a lively debate is going on about why the premium seems to be so high – investors get disproportionally rewarded for the additional risk they take. Explanations abound – maybe investors are more risk-averse than predicted by the models. Another explanation is that investors base the equity premium on one of the most successful financial markets. Dimson et al. calculated risk premiums worldwide in 2006, and estimated a 4.5–5% equity premium. In an experiment, pension fund executives were asked to give an estimate for financial indicators, deriving an equity risk premium of between –2 and +10.4% for the coming 20 years (Ambacht-sheer 2007). Besides being overly optimistic, this would have generally led to strong biases towards equities. In a broader setting, Graham and Harvey (2007) surveyed 7,300 American CFOs and distilled an expected equity premium of 3.2% per year. Overall, it is not clear how big the equity risk premium has been in the past, or how large it is today (Dimson et al. 2003). However, the assessment of what level the equity risk premium will be in the future largely determines a pension fund's allocation into equities. So guesstimates have to be made, depending very much on how you view the financial markets.

6.2.4   Longevity risk

Like the entire world's population, economic agents such as pension funds are exposed to mortality. The fact that life expectancy figures are increasing impacts pension funds, as it brings a risk of higher-than-expected payout ratios to the pensioners. This risk is referred to as longevity risk. The types of plans exposed to the greatest levels of longevity risk are defined-benefit pension plans and annuities, as they guarantee lifetime benefits for their participants. Even a very small discrepancy between actual and expected life expectancy figures can cause severe solvency problems for any pension fund.

Precise measurements of longevity risk are still not available, as various variables that impact longevity, such as innovations in medical treatments or the precise impact of medicines on life expectancies, are not or cannot be quantified. However, the previous years' ambiguity on longevity risk is decreasing due to the development of new measurements.

6.2.5   Illiquidity premium

Pension funds can choose to earn an illiquidity premium on their investments: an additional return for strategies of holding assets that are bought and sold in illiquid markets. For economists, illiquid markets are markets where buyers and sellers are thinly spread – it takes a while before a buyer is found, and chances are that the sale price is below what was expected. This typically applies to assets like real estate, private equity or infrastructure. In compensation, a pension fund is only prepared to hold on to such a security if the returns are higher than for more liquid securities. The longer the holding period, the greater the probability that these higher returns are structural. A belief about the illiquidity premium should therefore contain at least an idea about the holding period, for example:

Table 6.1   Illustration of risk premium investment beliefs

New Zealand Superannuation Fund – Investment Beliefs
The Fund's long-term investment horizon, combined with the fact that no outflows are required until at least 2020, means that the organization is extremely well positioned to capture illiquidity premium.[16]

Vanguard – Investment Philosophy – Belief #7
Risk has many dimensions, and investors should weigh "shortfall risk" – the possibility that a portfolio will fail to meet longer-term financial goals – against "market risk," or the chance that returns will fluctuate.[17]

6.3   Debates to be aware of

- Small changes in the assumptions tend to have large consequences for the portfolio and asset allocation. Proponents argue that there is less risk to equities over long investment periods – equities just need a long time to realize their return potential. However, common sense also dictates that while the *relative* risk might decrease over a longer time horizon, the *absolute* risk increases over time. Relative risk is usually brought forward in asset allocation studies in the shape of "we assume a long-term average equity return of 8%, moving between 7 and 9%". Absolute risk on the other hand is measured in hard currencies.
- Assuming that historical, realized risk premiums will help you in assessing future risk premiums is usually a tricky business. "Many new investment strategies are based on historical data that may no longer fit the circumstances", says Mike Housden of UBS Asset Management in the *Financial Times*.[18] Analysis of real estate or private equity returns may offer projections for the future, but fails to take into account the fact that historical real estate has been far less leveraged, or that the volume of new money allocated to private equity is likely to dampen returns. Other strategies have track records that are too brief to offer a useful prediction of what may happen as the investment cycle turns.
- According to David Blake from the Pensions Institute, reducing information like discount rates or risk premiums into single, easily interpreted measures leads to a false sense of certainty. Forecasts are only useful if we know the uncertainty around them; a single number cannot convey useful information about the distribution of future outcomes.[19]

7
Diversification

Summary

✓ Diversification – reducing risk by combining different assets with low correlation – is the classic backbone of investment management. New strategies, such as alternative investments and hedge funds, are increasingly being utilized as a tool for diversification.

✓ The concept has some serious drawbacks. Diversification advantages disappear every now and then, especially when investors need them the most – notably during crises. Trustees should be aware of this.

✓ Also, be aware that diversification is not necessarily achieved simply by adding new strategies to the portfolio. It does however become a robust part of the fund's toolkit if clear criteria are met.

7.1 Case study

Many investors would not consider swapping oil for equities a good diversification deal. Yet it paid off remarkably well for the Norwegians. Windfall wealth is a once-in-a-lifetime opportunity that ultimately challenges decision-makers on whether to use it for pet projects now, or save it and increase long-term wealth. The Dutch chose the former in the 1970s, spending income from natural gas and earning the dubious title of "the Dutch Disease" when inflation spun out of control. When the Norwegians hit oil in the 1980s, they took the latter approach and set oil income apart. It has helped the average Norwegian in the rankings. In the early 1970s, per capita wealth was $4,000, but today it is close to $35,000.[1] The Government set up the Government Petroleum Fund, later renamed Government Pension Fund Global, with the purpose of investing the country's oil wealth. Managing around $2,275 billion, it is invested almost entirely overseas and managed by the Norges Bank Investment Management (NBIM), which is the central bank's investment management department.[2]

Originally, the fund was invested the same way as the central bank's currency reserves, but in 1998, NBIM introduced equities with a 40% allocation in its portfolio, with the remainder in government bonds. Five years later, five emerging market countries were added to the equities universe; in 2002, fixed income was broadened from government to include non-government. Early 2007, it decided to increase its equities allocation to 60%, invest more in smaller companies, and considered hedge funds and private equity investments. On the one hand, the fund took on more risk, but this all depends on your point of view. Knut Kjaer, executive director of NBIM between 1998 and 2007, points out that oil price volatility has been much higher historically than equity or fixed income returns.[3] He calculates that one dollar invested in oil in 1900 would have increased to $2 in 2007, while the same dollar in equities would have yielded $376.

The strategic value of well thought-out diversification strategies cannot be underestimated. In Kentucky they learned this the hard way, when they failed to bring their diversification up to standard. The investment performance of the $17 billion Kentucky Retirement Systems (KRS) and $15.6 billion Kentucky Teachers Retirement System (KTRS) had been significantly underperforming similar systems across the country, according to a report conducted for Governor's Steve Beshear's public pension working group. The working group pinpointed failing diversification strategies and inadequate governance as the main culprits, and did some math. For the ten years ended June 30, 2008 Kentucky Retirement had an opportunity cost of $1.5 billion (8% of assets) and Kentucky Teachers, $3.5 billion (22% of assets), if both funds had adopted sound, unspectacular diversification strategies (Kentucky Public Pension Working Group 2008).

Kentucky Retirement Systems (KRS) invests funds and administers benefits for over 267,000 state and local government employees in Kentucky. These employees include state employees, state police officers, city and county employees, as well as non-teaching staff of local school boards and regional universities.

The ball started rolling when the Kentucky government hired an investment consultant in July 2008 to conduct an operational and governance review and recommend new investment policies to improve the investment performance of KRS. The review was prompted by its lagging returns. KRS, the largest fund, earned –5.8%, 4.6%, 6.2% and 4.5% for respectively

1, 3, 5, 10 years ending June 30, 2008, way below the actuarial assumed rate of return of 7.5%. Similar funds did not perform as badly, so the fund itself needed to be investigated. The investment consultant made some stark observations:

- "Home sweet home" applies to family, not investments. As of June 30, 2008, KTRS had 55% of the total portfolio, and 86% of the equity portfolio, allocated to the US equity market. Committing more than 50% of a portfolio to one single asset class exposes the investor to risks that can be avoided with a variety of assets classes.
- Conservative views on developments in the investment industry are not always a good thing. While the funds felt that peer comparisons were not that useful, paying attention to the competition might have paid off. Alternative assets, international equity and Treasury Inflation-Protected Securities (TIPS) were introduced from 2001 onwards, but at a very slow pace, increasing the gap with peers.
- Failing governance hits home. The investment consultant found that the investment committees were rather small, but especially objected to the fact that one of the funds did not require an investment expertise background for membership. Composition of the board, and bringing in investment expertise, is a crucial factor in governance.

The report recommended changes in investment committees and the development of new investment policies that would diversify assets, among other suggestions. Mike Burnside, Kentucky Retirement executive director, said the system has taken several steps recently to improve performance, such as hiring new consultants and investing more in emerging markets, private equity, real estate and other "areas we can diversify to enhance returns in the future." He noted in the industry journal PI Online that KRS now has an allocation more similar to the median fund.

7.2   Theory

Views on diversification have changed dramatically in the last decades. Pension funds in the 1970s were content with bonds and real estate, assets that were considered "safe". But returns were low, so funds moved progressively into equities, commercial property, foreign securities and derivatives. New technology made it possible: in the 1990s the pension fund industry experienced a makeover when the combination of Asset Liability Management (ALM) techniques, deregulation and portfolio optimization approaches gained ground, widening the scope of assets to invest in. The risks were higher, but so were the rewards. Additionally, higher returns brought down the relative costs of running the fund.

By the late 1990s the cult of equity had taken a firm hold. Pension funds increased their equity allocations dramatically (Ellison and Jolly 2008). Shell Pension Fund, managing over €11.7 billion in 1998, moved up to over 69% in equities;[4] other UK funds followed similar routes. The prospect of capital growth seemed too good to resist. Followers became disciples of the equity cult, placing strong belief in the equity risk premium. This belief was severely challenged in the early 2000s, when the IT and telecoms bubble in securities markets took its toll. In two years, the value of equities fell by over 50%.

To cope with this, diverging views emerged on diversification. On the one hand, some pension funds seemed to turn their back on these techniques and return to investing in bonds as their core approach, for example pension fund Boots, one of the largest 50 UK pension funds in 2001 when it pioneered a liability-driven approach.[5] On the other hand, other pension funds surged ahead, searching for new asset classes to further perfect their diversification. Alternative investments in particular benefited from this approach. However, after an initial recovery in the equity markets, the fall in 2001–2003 proved to be only a dress-rehearsal for 2008, when stock markets plummeted between 40–50% worldwide, stress-testing diversification to its limits.

Pension funds tend to stress the role of diversification more than asset managers (9.0% compared to 2.5%) as one of the few free lunches available in investments. Diversification is a simple, intuitively appealing approach to investing: figure out the combination of investment strategies and asset classes to yield the lowest possible risk, given the expected return that you aim for. Diversification is usually framed in a "mean variance" context: diversification among assets is an essential instrument for creating portfolios with a lower expected risk given the target return. Clearly, pension funds have become fond of diversifying. Since 2002 they have ventured into credits, emerging markets equity, infrastructure, hedge funds and private equity. The general idea was to be like Yale. The endowment fund produced enviable results, with net investment returns of 17.8% per year from 1998 until 2007.

Since the latest equity markets downturn in 2002–2004, and 2007–2008, views on diversification have shifted. An unpleasant surprise for many trustees and investment managers has been that diversification into alternative investments did not help the overall portfolio risk and return.

According to an old adage, correlation is the only thing that goes up in a downturn.[6] Low correlation as a measure of potential diversification does not hold up in periods of extreme volatility (Campbell et al. 2002). Most investment managers accept that correlation edges towards one during crises: however, alternative investments themselves also produced disappointing results.

Table 7.1   Example of risk diversification investment beliefs

---

New Zealand Superannuation Fund – Investment Beliefs
NZ Superannuation Fund believes that risk and return are strongly related and that diversification reduces total risk.[7]

Vanguard – Investment Philosophy – Belief #2
Broad diversification, with exposure to all parts of the stock and bond markets, reduces risk.[8]

Universities Superannuation Scheme (USS)
USS Investments believes that the "emphasis on the risk-reducing benefit of diversification is a fundamental investment principle."[9]

Still, investment managers increasingly look to add new – alternative – investments to bolster diversification advantages (Fabozzi et al. 2005), which mitigate these risks to a large extent. However, there is no point in adding new strategies and further diversifying, if the investment does not offer a genuinely different source of return, or if the asset is already overvalued. In other words, the hurdle for new investments counting as a true "diversifier" has increased substantially (Table 7.2), and if these investments are true diversifiers, their relative size in the investment portfolio is limited.[10]

Consider the last investments your fund made; do they measure up to the following criteria?

1. *Reduce overall portfolio risk*. Whenever two imperfectly correlated assets are placed in a portfolio, there is an opportunity to earn a greater return at the same risk, or earn the same return at a lower risk. The correlation between the new asset and the assets in the portfolio should reflect a sufficiently different pattern of returns; and the allocation of the new asset should be sizeable enough to matter.
2. *Hedge against adverse asset pricing shocks*. If there are extreme price movements in the financial markets, will the new asset's lack of correlation disappear and is diversification suspended? Or does the new asset provide a really new, independent economic source of return where it is

Table 7.2 Diversification strategies added to the investment portfolio since 1980

Strategy	Description	Correlation with other assets	Since
Commodities	Investing in economic inputs: physical assets (food, grains and metals) or energy (electricity, oil).	Weak – commodities are early in the economic cycle. Another attractive feature is its positive correlation with inflation, hence a favourite of pension funds.	Late 1990s
Private equity	Buying into companies not listed on stock exchanges, ranging from young and emerging to old and mature.	Correlation with equities depends on leverage (increasing risk profile) and type of private equity (for example, large buy-outs differ little from equities, venture capital differs a lot).	1980s
Infrastructure	Long-term investments or project development of roads, airports, harbours etc.	Specialized form of real estate. Especially attractive for long-term investors when income can be adjusted to inflation and regulation does not allow many new rival projects.	2000s
Catastrophe bonds	Insurance policies where investors earn an above-average income stream, but may lose the principal when the insurer pays out in case of a catastrophe such as a hurricane, earthquake or storm.	Weak – economic downturns will not bring forth more natural disasters (although a nasty disaster may generate a degree of economic gloom).	2000s
Music rights	Earn a steady stream of income with music rights that have to be paid to artists.	Weak – the work of artists has nothing to do with the state of the economy, so it will not be correlated with other assets.	Dutch ABP started investing in 2006.

Table 7.2 Diversification strategies added to the investment portfolio since 1980 – *continued*

Strategy	Description	Correlation with other assets	Since
Carbon credits	Creation of a market for mandatory trading of carbon dioxide emissions within the Kyoto Protocol. The London financial marketplace has established itself as the center of the carbon finance market.	In theory, weak correlation, but in practice, high volatility; returns are politically driven in anticipation of changing caps on the volume of traded carbon credits. There is also a "political" correlation: in economic downturns, governments might loosen their carbon emission reduction policies to help industry, lowering the prices of carbon credits.[11]	A market valued at $60 billion in 2007. The voluntary offset market is projected to grow to about $4 billion by 2010.
Hedge funds	Earn steady stream of income from fund whosemanagers can, without restrictions, buy or sell any assets, and bet on falling as well as rising assets.	In theory, weak correlation with traditional assets. Image tarnished after 2007 when hedge funds showed negative results – too much leverage and indistinguishable strategies left them exposed to normal (market) risks.	Pioneered in the late 1940s,[12] the industry took off in the late 1980s, estimated at more than $1 trillion in 2007.
Life Settlements	Buying up second-hand life assurance policies of elderly and dying policyholders.	Weak correlation with traditional assets, seen as hedge against longevity risk.	Mainly developed in the United States, slow adaptation in other countries, mainly ethical considerations.

ex ante unlikely that it moves in step with the other assets? A simple question, but hard to answer. Research shows for example that country equity markets offer less diversification in down-markets than in up-markets. The same is true for global industry returns, individual stocks, hedge fund returns, international bonds etc. Similarly, international diversification seems to work during good times, when it is least needed, but disappears during falling markets, when it is most needed. Maybe the only bright spot here is that asset correlation *within* countries decreases during periods of market turbulence (Chua et al. 2008).

3. *Achieve high absolute and risk-adjusted returns.* Is the new asset able to bring home some bacon relative to the major asset classes in the portfolio? The appropriate measure to use is the Sharpe ratio, measuring the excess return above the risk-free rate per unit of risk (Sharpe 1994).

4. *Hedge against unexpected inflation or deflation.* Conventional wisdom has held that assets like real estate and long-term bonds hedge against inflation. However, except for inflation-linked bonds, many assets have a complicated relationship with inflation. Inflation elicits different responses; real estate contracts can have a standard clause where rents are corrected for inflation, creating an adequate inflation hedge. Many assets per definition provide a partial inflation hedge. Inflation may raise future cash flows, but this is partially offset: inflation also increases the nominal interest rate to discount the cash flows, decreasing the overall valuation. Also, the fact that there is a historical correlation with inflation should not simply be extrapolated into the future. Unforeseen consequences can always spoil the future. For example, thanks to the enormous success of Wal-Mart, few retail chains are now able to pass on increased inflation to customers; Wal-Mart alone is credited with reducing inflation in the 1990s in the US at a rate of 1% per year (Emek 2004).

5. *Reflect the overall investment universe.* A portfolio with 50% equities and 50% bonds might be called a balanced portfolio, but it is definitely not a reflection of the investment universe. This implies – in theory – that any portfolio that does not include for example private equity takes an implicit bet that a portfolio without private equity yields better returns.

6. *Deliver strong cash flows to the investor.* Pension funds are all about liquidity, and one of their major concerns is the creation of a stream of cash flows that to a large degree offsets the pension payments to be made. Investments with strong cash flows provide a natural hedge against pension liabilities, which are basically a set of future cash payouts anyway.

7. *Full circle*. Moving into new investment opportunities might be a tempting way to diversify your portfolio and yield a lower risk profile. However, a new asset can be valued thoroughly only after it has experienced a full blown up and downswing; a so-called "full circle". Many new alternative investments have not started to go "full circle" yet; hedge funds until recently being one of them. Up until 2007, we had only seen the upward potential for hedge funds, giving the investment industry no insight into the downside. Because hedge funds have been showing negative results since 2007, we are now better able to assess a realistic risk/return forecast for such investments.

7.3 Debates to be aware of

- Our point here is that adding new strategies does not necessarily achieve diversification. With hindsight, many alternative investment strategies suffered from two problems (*Economist* 2008). First, the success of many new strategies was boosted by the same factors: low interest rates and robust economic growth. That encouraged investors to use leverage to enhance returns. Some alternative investments share more factors: private equity gives investors exposure to the same kind of risk as quoted public equity, albeit with added leverage. When prospects deteriorated, investors were forced to sell all those asset classes simultaneously. Secondly, some of the asset classes are rather small. This illiquidity is attractive (see Figure 6.1) since it offers higher returns. As more investors get involved, the market becomes liquid, and the higher return is eroded. However, when everyone tries to sell, illiquidity rears its ugly head – there are no buyers to be found and prices tumble. This is very unpleasant when pension funds have to value their investment at market value.
- Diversification runs up against natural barriers. Investing in index funds is cheap. But diversifying in recent years has meant buying into alternative asset classes, costing more to trade, with higher management fees and expenses that eat into pension-fund returns. This is especially relevant if your fund is not the first one to invest in the new alternative asset. Dutch railway pension fund SPF Beheer deliberately steered away from hedge funds in 2005 when it concluded that the net return and reduction in risk by adding hedge funds to their portfolio did not offset the high costs of hedge funds. John van Markwijk, investment director at SPF, points out an additional issue: you have to be among the first to enter the new alternative strategies; there is no point in joining the herd later on. Once other investors enter, investment returns run the risk of

being eroded partly due to the increased supply of capital, but also because investors have moved up in the investment cycle.[13]

• Beliefs about the concept of asset diversification are shifting. Consider the Indianapolis-based Lumina Foundation, founded in 2000 to help people in education beyond high school through grants and policy education.[14] Nathan Fisher, Chief Investment Officer, managing $1.2 billion, organizes his portfolio by looking at how each asset class behaves in terms of risk, return and diversification. The portfolio is divided into four categories: growth drivers, diversifiers, inflation hedges and deflation hedges. There are no target allocations, rather broad ranges. Fisher acknowledges that this is a new way of thinking, saying that he wants "Treasury bonds for protection; [...] I don't want them for high yield". The appealing aspect for investors is that it allows them to be as opportunistic in investments as they like – or as the fund's risk appetite allows them to be. The delineation of categories depends on the fund's preferences, and is risk-based. Essentially, the fund rebalances its risk profile rather than rebalancing allocation in classes. The Lumina approach is novel, but it will probably have to share the innovation award with Bridgewater, managing approximately $72 billion in global investments for a wide array of institutional clients, which pioneered its "All Weather" portfolio. Some of the praise should also go to Asset Liability Management (ALM) consultants, who increasingly tend to examine how the investment portfolio performs in one of four regimes: low-high economic growth, and low-high inflation.

8
Investment Horizon

Summary

✓ Pension liabilities have a very long duration. Therefore pension funds typically have a long investment horizon, covering several decades.

✓ The main advantage of long-term investing is that it enables the fund to reap the benefits of time diversification, as the relative deviation around the long-term return decreases.

✓ Academics are not quite convinced that investing with a long-term horizon pays off, as it does not guarantee against losses. In absolute dollars, the possible deviation actually increases over time.

✓ Pension funds should find an adequate balance between short-term and long-term investing, and be aware that asset managers have a short-term focus.

8.1 Case study

Unsurprisingly, the style of investing that appeals to the French meets their taste for grand, long-term designs, exemplified by the Parisian Boulevards, the High Speed TGV train or the Channel Tunnel. The latest grand design is on combating ageing, setting up a reserve fund with the challenge of developing a strategic vision on long-term investing, and developing an appropriate investment style. French *Fonds De Reserve Pour Les Retraites* (FRR) was founded in 2001, with assets of $34.5 billion at end 2007, contributing to the funding needs of three pay-as-you-go (PAYG) retirement plans: the Old Age Fund, the Fund for self-employed retailers and business heads, and the Fund for skilled tradespersons.[1] Under the terms of the parliamentary act, the FRR will make no financial contribution to these pension funds prior to 2020, and that is what makes it special. The FRR is created to serve the pension system, taking on a portion of the expenses of basic private sector plans as of 2020, when the full impact of the demographic shock will begin to be felt. The fund's termination date is also known – somewhere between 2040 and 2050.

The part of the projected PAYG shortfalls that the Fund will finance from 2020 onwards will depend on the funding it receives until this date. Up to now, the fund has been receiving a varying annual contribution from the government, ranging from €5.5 billion in 2002 to €1.5 billion in 2006. Financing comes from surpluses from the National Old Age Insurance Fund for Wage Earners and the Old Age Solidarity Fund, additional taxes on private assets, and contributions from savings banks and the Deposit and Securities Fund plus infrequent cash injections. Some funding also comes from asset sales: starting in 2000, the bulk of the revenue generated by the sale of licenses for third generation cellular telephones was also to be transferred to the FRR.[2]

Translating a longer-term horizon into portfolio management is rather more difficult. Judging by the asset allocation, it is apparently not in this case about earning the illiquidity premium by investing heavily in alternative assets. Roughly 60% is invested in equities and 30% in bonds, skewed towards the euro zone. The remaining 10% is allocated to alternative assets. Here too, the French adhere to the grand design. In FRR's annual report, the directors argue that as a long-term investor, the FRR should have a positive impact on the economy:

- The FRR helps improve the allocation of savings on a national basis by increasing the portion of these savings invested in equities. Many studies indicate that French savings – especially household savings – are not as a whole optimally invested. For example, only 15% of life insurance assets are invested in equities. In contrast, the FRR's target weight for equities in its portfolio is 60%.
- The FRR acts as a market stabilizer. Unlike investors looking for short-term returns, the FRR does not constantly adjust its investment strategy in response to day-to-day market fluctuations. Freed of all liquidity constraints, it can support its financial decisions until they pay off.
- The FRR can incorporate sources of long-term value into its strategy that markets are not always able to take advantage of. For example, by implementing a socially responsible investment policy, the FRR can consider

factors other than financial ones to improve its investment decisions (see Chapter 14 on sustainability).

The first two objectives are difficult to measure, and might only become relevant when FRR's size relative to the French economy and the financial markets becomes substantial. The third is more tangible. True to its intentions, FRR has been active in implementing Socially Responsible Investments (SRI). More interestingly, it has also taken steps to implement corporate governance and engagement, in what observers expect to become a test case on how truly independent the fund really is.

8.2 Theory

Financial markets generally react with a lag, and if they react, they over-react. In today's volatile markets, pension funds have been hailed as long-term investors: investors with an investment horizon covering several

Table 8.1 Problems and opportunities behind short-term and long-term investing

	Short-term investment horizon	Long-term investment horizon
Problems	• Narrow investment criteria • Excessive focus on near term returns • Excessive focus on relative returns to asset-based index, rather than liability-based benchmarks • Short-term performance appraisal • Short-term investment mandates, for liquid asset categories	• Governance: boards can direct accountability into the future (just wait), and the past (e.g. the decision had a horizon of ten years to be fully evaluated) • Long-term strategies based on limited assumptions – risk and illiquidity premiums
Opportunities	• Manoeuvring scope to exploit temporary inefficiencies for asset managers • Earn excess return by consciously investing in emerging trends	• Invest in intergenerational assets • Focus on absolute returns and liability based benchmarks • Exploit diversification advantages • Low cost strategies create impact

Source: Partly based on Guyatt (2008)

decades. For pension investors, 6.4% of pension funds' investment beliefs address the investment horizon (see Table 4.1). Investment horizon beliefs, in combination with beliefs about risk premiums, have been the main drivers behind the thrust towards equities since the late 1990s. When choosing between a short-term and long-term investment horizon, both approaches have their own problems and opportunities (Table 8.1).

An investment horizon is the period of time during which a fund can hold on to its investments before it has to liquidate (part of) these, due to projected cash outflows in the form of pension payments from that period onwards. By their very nature, pension funds have to find a balance between the short-term and long-term horizon. Pension funds generally appoint external parties, usually investment managers, for managing their investments. Their focus is however on short-horizon processes and predicting and exploiting temporary securities pricing discrepancies. Investment strategies based on short-term strategies are zero-sum games before expenses (Ambachtsheer 2007). Pension fund managers must inevitably be concerned with short-term returns; part of the benchmarking process is fundamental to their fiduciary duty (Clark and Hebb 2004).

The main idea is that a longer horizon allows the investor to profit more from time diversification. Longer holding periods reduce the error of the estimated returns. The theoretical argument in favor of time diversification stems from Bernouilli's law of large numbers. On the one hand, you might decline a single tossing gamble that offers a $2 gain on a heads and a $1 loss on a tails; on the other hand a game of ten repeats seems quite attractive. Choose a long enough sequence, and success might actually materialize. It is this form of reasoning that underpins Zvi Bodie's argument on time diversification that "the riskiness of stocks diminishes with the length of an investor's time horizon" (Bodie 1995). Statistically, the longer the investment period, the smaller the standard error of the estimated return becomes. Intuitively, if investors hold risky assets for long enough, they should weather the ups and downs of the market and earn the risk premium.

In theory, this period should be long enough to encapsulate peaks and troughs of the investment cycle, or capture the additional return of undervalued stocks. Thinking about investing over the cycle introduces a fallacy with trustees: the inevitability of *mean reversion*. A normal remark is: "Now that we have experienced five years of negative returns, positive returns are bound to come in the next years". People have a poor intuitive understanding of the characteristics of random processes and how to predict future processes (Shefrin 2000). Consider a coin-tossing experiment, where the "run" so far is five times heads, and the question is what the likely outcome for the next five tosses should be. Chances are that trustees will point to five tails as the most likely possible outcome, reasoning that this is due to the law of averages. A statistician however would not be so sure and identify two to three tails as more likely: the future is not indebted to the past in any way.

Pension liabilities have a very long duration. The discounted weighted average time to payment is generally more than 15 years, and payment of some of the liabilities may not fall due for many decades. It is therefore appropriate for pension funds to take a long-term view in setting strategic asset allocation (SAA) and investment policies. Proponents argue that there is less risk to equities over long investment horizons, often referred to as time diversification. This notion is the popular rationale for advocating high levels of equity investments (Cooper and Bianco 2003).

However, time diversification is a complex issue. While it seems valid to assume that the *relative* deviation around the long-term return decreases, the possible deviation in *absolute* dollar terms actually increases over time. So it's a matter of how you frame it: if you're a believer in equities and long-term investing you show the relative figures; if you're not so sure, you go with the absolute numbers (Figure 8.1). Equity investments are usually

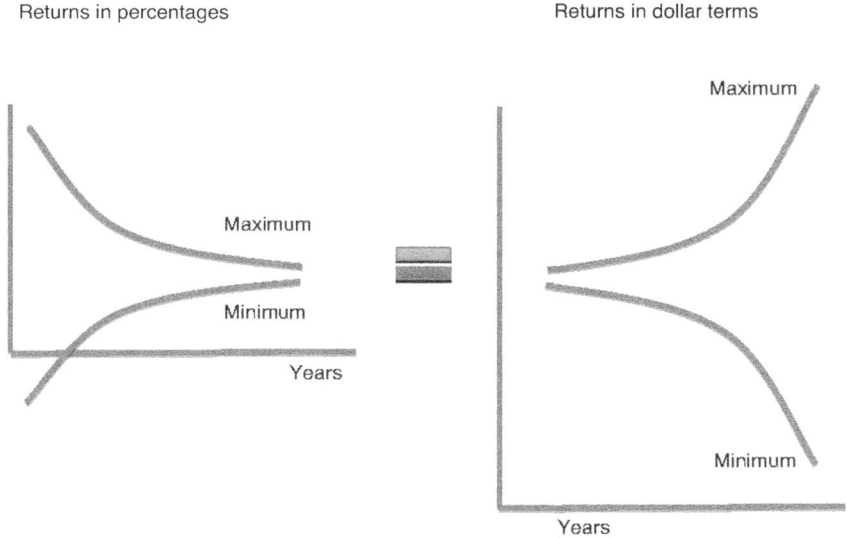

Figure 8.1   Framing benefits of investment horizon in relative or absolute returns

riskier over long periods of time. The argument that the relative standard error of returns decreases also applies to other investments.

Second, time diversification is usually intertwined (or confused) with mean reversion – the implicit belief that securities revert to long-term average trend growth. The empirical evidence for this is not strong, and basically implies a risky bet on contrarian strategies: "Buy low and sell high" is based on this concept, implying that you should buy when prices and valuations of securities seem cheap, and sell when they are high. However, when someone argues that a security is cheap, then it immediately follows that he has a higher price in mind that seems to better reflect the true value. So you earn money by buying the security, and hoping that the valuation reverts back to what you think the mean is. The flaw in this reasoning is that we do not have an idea of what the true value is, short of liquidating the underlying company. Investors in the Japanese market have lost money over two decades, basically because after each decline in stock market prices it seemed more likely that securities would revert back to their "true" valuation. We now know that this true value can also decline. Exit mean reversion for the Japanese stock market.

Furthermore, when researchers take a historical view of the stock market, several issues emerge. For starters, having a long investment horizon is not a guarantee of positive returns. There is no such thing as a long-term average return and risk on equities, bonds or cash. It is very time dependent: the choice of starting and ending point for the holding period matters. Time diversification, as Fisher and Statman (1999) call it, does not provide a guarantee against losses; stocks can go down as easily as they go up, even in the long run. Dimson et al. (2003) calculate real equity returns for portfolios between 1900 and 2003, varying the holding period and starting date, and show that real equity return in the US is positive for *all* portfolios once the investment horizon is 20 years, but this horizon would be at least 75 years in Italy. Italy is not an exception; while the US, Canada, Australia and Denmark never experienced a negative result over any interval of 20 years, 11 other countries were negative from time to time.

It is interesting to consider the time and gains needed to compensate for a (significant) loss on the stock market. Consider the Wall Street Crash of 1929, the most devastating stock market crash of the US taking into account the full extent and duration of its fallout. On Monday October 28, also known as "Black Monday", investors decided to get out of the market en masse, resulting in a record day loss for the Dow of 13%. The next day, "Black Tuesday", Dow lost another 12%. After some fluctuations the Dow reached its lowest level of the 20th century on July 8, 1932. The Dow closed at 41.22 that day, concluding a shattering 89% decline from the peak. This was the lowest the stock market had been since the 19th century and it did not return to pre-1929 levels until 23 November 1954 – a 25-year period. As Richard Salsman states: "Anyone who bought stocks in mid-1929 and held onto them saw most of his or her adult life pass by before getting back to even." Considering Figure 8.2, this is no surprise, as a 90% loss requires a 900% gain to compensate for the loss. This means that a 50% loss, as occurred with the credit crunch of 2008, can only be compensated by a 100% gain over time.

The investment industry is naive in this regard; long-term investing is usually framed as "if you had invested $1 in the stock market in 1929

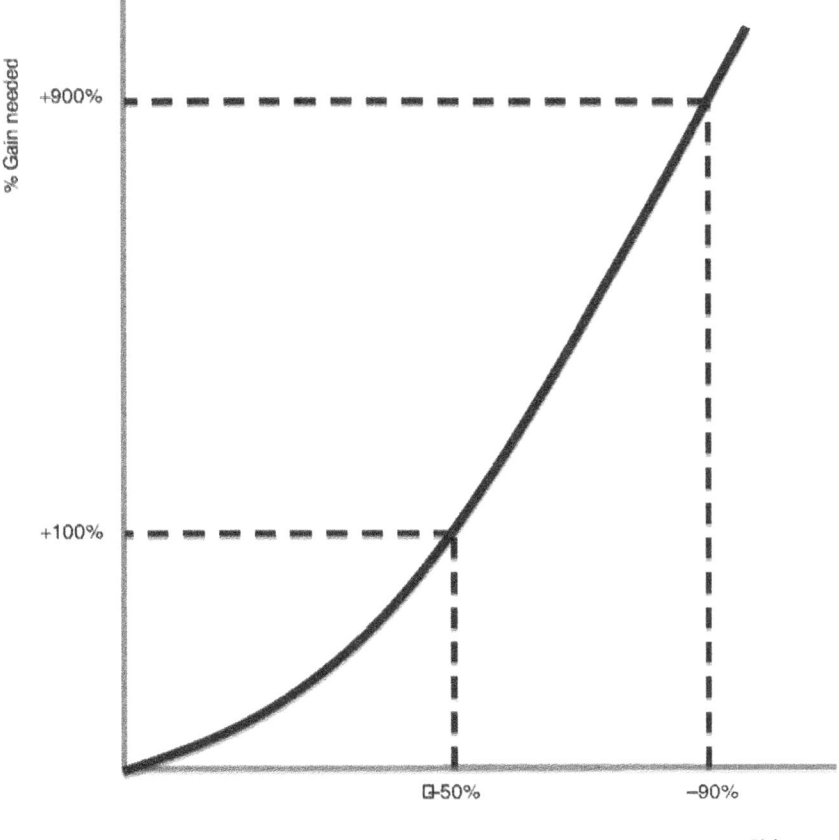

Figure 8.2   Percentage losses and gains needed to break even

Table 8.2   Illustration of investment horizon beliefs

Pictet assumes that "value measures give no indication about the short-term return of a financial asset, but valuation is central to the long-term (five years and more) return estimate." Also, "in the short run, the economy can be better predicted on the basis of the financial markets than the other way around."[3]

"Investing is for meeting long-term goals; saving is for meeting short-term goals."[4] Therefore, Vanguard advises: "Begin by making an asset allocation decision that gives heavy weight to the time-horizon of the investment objective."

Pension fund PGGM aims to: "Use its strength as a long-term investor. [...] "Because pension investments have a long-term horizon, we select investments for our client which generate a high return in the long term."[5]

---

and simply kept your money there all the way through to 2008, your investment would have grown to $80,000". The implicit belief here is that through a buying and holding investment strategy, everything works out in the end. This is a dangerous notion though for two reasons. First, the investor in 1926 was a totally different one, operating in a market, economy and political environment only remotely familiar to us today, and this cannot be compared in a simple metric with our time. Second, swings in returns severely test the determination to hang on for the long term and require a strong governance structure to hold onto a high equities allocation after a sharp downturn, like the one experienced in 2008. The long-term advantages of long-term investing are rational and appealing, but only a few funds and managers are able to reap the advantages.

8.3   Debates to be aware of

Markets in turmoil require pension funds as long-term investors to think carefully about what long-term investing really means: is it simply holding on through the turbulence, or thinking carefully about changes in their asset strategies? They have to strike a balance between investing with a long-term perspective and making implementation decisions quickly. Here is where the difference between long-term and short-term correlations starts to matter. If you take a ten-year view, it still looks as though property, commodities and private equity offer some diversification benefits. While correlations still serve up a free lunch, this decreases in size. Financial engineering has led to the development of instruments that blur the traditional boundaries between asset classes. A typical equity manager used to invest in equities only, but has acquired a wide range of new instruments like futures, options, swaps, and other equity derivatives. He is now able to trade on most global exchanges; together with his colleagues' activities, this results in a massive flow of funds switching between exchanges every day. The demarcation line between asset classes and regions has faded. As a result, the correlation between regions and asset classes has increased gradually and steadily (cf. Gupta and Straatman 2005).

Investment managers believe that focusing on the longer-term horizon has the additional benefit of avoiding a potential zero-sum game. Guyatt (2005) surveyed 180 professionals associated with the Marathon Club, a group formed to encourage pension funds, endowments and other institutional investors to be more long-term in their thinking and actions. Thirty percent of respondents believed that lengthening the investment horizon would improve corporate behavior and ultimately portfolio performance, while 26% also viewed a longer horizon as an opportunity to integrate extra financial information and thus improve the valuation of securities and assets. Twelve percent added another element, namely that withstanding short-term market trends and cycles is important.

9
The Investment Process: Impact and Focus of Decisions

Summary

✓ The investment process outlines the steps in creating a portfolio while emphasizing the sequence of actions involved. Asset allocation impacts performance and risk to a large degree.

✓ Focus matters for governance: It is necessary to agree on clear roles and functions. For example, the board of trustees performs strategic asset allocation, while tactical asset allocation is performed by the investment staff.

✓ An emerging view is that traditional asset allocation should be abandoned, and categories should be clustered according to the underlying risk/return factors.

9.1   Endowed with focus

In the endowment industry, investors closely watch and hope to emulate funds like Yale and Harvard. For the pension industry, the Canadian Ontario Teachers Pension Plan (OTPP) surely fits into the same league. With a clear view of what the plan's main success drivers were, the fund transformed itself into a leading pension fund worldwide.

Leading the way to shape future investment processes is not without risk however, as Canadian OTPP experienced when the fund with three private equity partners proposed to buy Bell Canada Enterprises for the staggering amount of $52 billion. The sheer size, as well as the hands-on approach in buying companies directly, and the (economic) risks attached, created a lot of public attention. The difficult deal for OTPP points to one of the drawbacks of being possibly the world's most actively managed pension fund; it certainly would not have faced such public scrutiny if it had invested in index funds.[1] But then again, the fund probably would not have earned such impressive returns above its benchmark. Between 1990 and the end of 2008 it managed to outperform its annual benchmark by 2.1% on average.[2]

Ontario Teachers' Pension Plan is the largest single-profession pension fund in Canada, and currently holds assets with a net worth of C$106 billion ($100 billion). It is an independent corporation, with 600 employees, working with its sponsors (the Ontario government and the Ontario Teachers' Federation) to make investments for the pensions of the province's teachers. There are 271,000 teachers, both working and retired, currently involved in the plan. Like many pension funds, OTPP is struggling with a shortfall of $19 billion,[3] because there are only 1.6 working teachers for every pensioner. While the problem is hardly unique, OTPP's innovative investing approach is. Its investments since 1990 have achieved an average annual rate of return of 9.6%, and cover a diverse range of sectors, notably infrastructure, utilities and telecoms. OTPP experienced a dramatic transformation in the early 1990s, when the fund became independent from the Canadian government.

Lamoureux was the first CEO of the fund, formed in 1990 from the government-run Teachers' Superannuation Plan. In subsequent years, Teachers' morphed from a plan restricted to investing in non-marketable provincial debentures (since its inception in 1917 to its remodeling in 1990), to managing all of its assets directly as of 1990. The fund developed a clear focus that sets it apart today:

- Lamoureux's adage that the fund should be run like a business has shaped the governance of the fund. Eschewing the union and political appointees who dominate most European and American pension fund boards, the OTPP board draws heavily from the business world. OTPP concentrates on generating investment returns in a similarly businesslike way. While sustainability criteria are incorporated into decision-making as risk factors, it clearly warns plan members that the fund is not in place to reflect their individual concerns and views.[4] On the other hand, following up on the business philosophy, the fund takes a strong stance on corporate governance, and even bought in 2007 the leading US governance analysis and proxy voting firm Glass Lewis.
- It is almost entirely internally managed, using a small number of outside managers for specific purposes. It draws on a highly qualified internal staff to generate additional returns to the benchmarks.

- OTTP is an active pension fund, with its investments heavily skewed towards private investments, notably private equity and infrastructure. For Teachers' purposes, the risks of the private equity investments are counterbalanced by the longer-lived and more stable cash flows of the traditional infrastructure assets. Ontario Teachers was one of the first pension funds to invest directly in infrastructure assets.[5] The long life of the investment and its low volatility in returns offsets the greater volatility of the private equity investments with shorter life spans. "The infrastructure investments hedge the risks of the more highly levered deals," says Leech, succeeding Lamoreux as CEO. This underlines the stark commitment of OTPP to running its pension fund like a business, and its commitment to private investments.

9.2   Theory

The investment process outlines the steps in creating a portfolio, and emphasizes the sequence of actions involved: from understanding the investor's risk preferences to asset allocation, and from selection to performance evaluation. The investment process provides a structure that allows stakeholders to see the source of different investment strategies and choices within the investment portfolio.

An investment process combines all the necessary steps to move from conceptualizing the investor's mission to realizing the returns in relation to the risk attitude and to prior set goals. The investment process emphasizes the different components that are needed for an investment strategy to be successful.

Pension funds, more than asset managers, tend to articulate the *impact of management decisions* they ought to make within the investment process, with greater emphasis on their fiduciary responsibilities along the way. Funds tend to concentrate on strategic asset allocation, rather than tactical asset allocation. The board of trustees performs strategic asset allocation, while tactical asset allocation is performed by the investment staff. Trustees set target allocations along the main asset categories like equities, fixed income, private equity and real estate; the investment staff should further drill down to sub-asset class.

The goal of the strategic asset allocation is to create as efficient as possible a market exposure to realize the targeted long-term returns within the set risk limits. A strategic asset allocation does not attempt to beat the market; its goal is to track a combination of market indices with as little deviation as possible (Anson 2005). The strategic asset allocation portfolio created is dubbed "beta". Anson notes that the beta portfolio is linear in its performance. The returns rise and fall with the financial markets.

The focus on asset allocation is a key element, reflecting research which shows that the decision on allocating assets within a portfolio may play a greater role in shaping risk and performance than the tactical movements of holdings within asset classes (Brinson et al. 1986; Brinson et al. 1991). The conclusions of the studies of Brinson et al. introduced one of the classic yardsticks: almost 94% of the differences in returns of institutionally managed pension funds are determined by the allocation of assets.

Blake et al. (1999) added an interesting twist to this line of studies. In the 1990s they repeated the studies in depth among UK pension funds and again confirmed that asset allocation determined the bulk of the variation between returns. But they also looked at the industry. At the time of their investigation, more than 80% of institutional assets were being managed by five large fund managers. In a market characterized by few suppliers, portfolios were likely to be dominated by a small number of external fund managers who, in addition, had an incentive to remain closely aligned to each other to reduce the risk of relative underperformance. A pension fund's performance is increasingly monitored in terms of its solvency, represented by its inverse measure, the ratio of assets to liabilities. While this adds a layer to the decisions to be made, the main conclusions from studies like Blake et al. still hold up.

Table 9.1   Illustration of management decision investment beliefs

---

AXA Rosenberg believes that "it is extremely difficult to time markets or sectors consistently. So instead we create portfolios that have similar characteristics to the benchmarks selected by our clients and aim to outperform using stock selection."[6]

T. Rowe Price "does not seek to achieve excess returns through volatile, short-term investment strategies or securities [...]. Rather, we pursue a highly disciplined, risk-controlled investment process aimed at achieving consistent, long-term returns."[7]

Ontario Teachers Pension Plan does "not get involved in the day-to-day operations of the widely-held companies in which we invest. A company's management and board of directors are responsible for the benefit of all shareholders to ensure compliance with the laws and standards of the countries in which they operate."[8]

9.3 Debates to be aware of

For a decision to be effective, its impact should (eventually) overtake noise. A misapplication of decision-making is micro management. For example, using an asset liability management model to recommend a change of 1% in strategic long-term asset allocation weighting might seem very clever – probably inspired by the idea of improving risk-return trade-offs in the portfolio, but does not in practice make sense. No model can have that much precision; the markets are just too noisy to justify this (Gray 1997). Investors run the risk of over-quantification, and overestimating their capacity to manage risk and return, with a blinkered focus on the impact of measurable concepts on the grounds that "what gets measured gets managed."

The strategic asset allocation decision can be "blurred" by learning experiences and political gestures. Adding an allocation of 0.7% for hedge funds or micro-finance investments seems like a big step, but it is barely visible in the performance and risk attribution. Larger pension funds tend to group these investments together and re-label them "portfolio of strategies" (PGGM) or "innovation platform" (ABP).

There is no clear-cut definition of what constitutes an asset class. In its 1995 annual report, Yale Endowment observes that "because investment management involves as much art as science, qualitative considerations play an extremely important role in portfolio decisions. The definition of an asset class is quite subjective, requiring precise distinctions where none exist."[9] A rule of thumb is that assets should be distinguished on the basis of their economic exposure, and should not be defined by their historical correlations (Greer 1997). New asset classes are introduced on a regular basis; in some cases the asset is a "spin-off" from the traditional strategic asset allocation. Think of currencies as an asset class – they used to be part of foreign exposure in the portfolio, but owing to financial innovation, they are now grouped and managed separately.[10]

An emerging trend is for consultants and investment managers to argue that traditional asset allocation should be abandoned, and categories should be clustered according to the underlying risk/return factors. The main driver behind this idea is that asset delineations are becoming blurred anyhow. No more strategic asset allocation but *beta-alpha management*; separately managing the overall risk and return the fund needs by simply investing in the markets (beta), and additional returns from savvy managers and strategies, capitalizing on skill (alpha). This seems like a good idea, since it appeals to the basics of real diversification. However, common sense says that this is rephrasing the problem that we have addressed under the diversification belief. What constitutes real diversification? Adding strategies with new risk/return factors – is that not the same as defining an asset class?

Decision-making and impact focus decisions are not always aligned. The academic evidence shows that asset allocation rather than good stock picking is the main determinant of the performance of the fund. Many trustees do not take asset allocation advice, but make those decisions for themselves. They split the fund between different (specialist) managers, deciding the proportions for each sort of asset, or alternatively award the fund to managers with target guidelines for exposure in different asset classes. "Maybe instead trustees should spend their fee budget on asset allocation advice rather than on manager selection advice", says John Redwood, arguing that a fund needs an adviser on asset allocation to alert them to big changes that may require a rethink of their strategy.[11] While lagging performance of active managers alerted trustees to the dire consequences of the credit crunch late 2007, few funds have seized on the warning signals to review the strategic asset allocation.

10
Risk Management

Summary

✓ Though risk *diversification* is oftentimes stressed as one of the key investment beliefs of pension funds, risk *management* may well be one of the least appreciated ones.

✓ External asset managers may opt for high-risk alternatives as they, in many cases, increase the chances of outperformance and subsequently a performance fee.

✓ Therefore, trustees need to think more about the risks they manage and the extent to which they can mitigate the risk, especially when the assets are managed outside the pension fund.

✓ Sound risk management should anticipate the risk of financial crises instead of reasoning it away. As volatility in financial markets has been rising, we should train to cope with crises and incorporate crises in our quantitative models.

✓ Risk management incurs the danger of over-quantification: the illusion that if the risk is quantified, it can also be managed; *measurement should not dominate meaning.*

10.1   Case study

Two decades ago it used to be easy to run an asset allocation strategy for a UK pension fund: buy some bonds and a bit of property, but the largest slice of the pie – approximately 70% – should be in equity.[1] However, when risk management became the core of the thinking, exciting changes were bound to happen. In 2001, the pension fund of Boots, the UK pharmacy-led and beauty retailer shook up the UK pension scene announcing that it was switching all of its £2.3 billion worth of pension assets over a 15-month period from equities into long-term bonds.[2]

John Ralfe, former Head of Corporate Finance at Boots, ensured that these bonds had the highest credit rating, so that Boots pensioners should not worry about credit risk. Ralfe explained that the move to bonds was purely about reducing the risks for various stakeholders of Boots.[3] To start with, it increased security for the pension scheme members as bonds move more in line with the pension liabilities than equities do. Furthermore, bonds are less risky and in combination with the healthy funding of the Boots pension fund at that moment, the probability of a secure pension was larger than with equities. Moreover the switch led to a reduction in costs from £10 million to only £250,000 a year,[4] as the fund needed less management and faced less transaction costs with this buy-and-hold bond strategy.

Regarding risks, Boots took on a rather broad view since the risks faced by its pension fund were clearly viewed as a part of the sponsoring company, which in turn has its private shareholders.[5] Ralfe claims that by holding equities in its pension fund, a company is doing nothing its private share-holders cannot do directly, more tax efficiently and more transparently themselves.[6]

Although Boots' move seems to be a rigorous one, its timing turned out to be perfect as interest rates declined and stock markets subsequently faltered;[7] Ralfe: "We cashed in our chips while we were ahead."[8] Near the end of 2002, it was estimated that the remarkable switch made the fund £700 million better off.

However, in the long term, being fully invested in bonds can also lead to the need for higher contributions as bonds feature less return potential than equities.

Another fund that took (risk) measures in good times is the Dutch Rabobank Pension Fund (RPF). Just like its sponsoring company, Rabobank, a Dutch international financial services provider, RPF puts a lot of emphasis on dealing with different risks.[9] Its central goal is to control the risk of not being able to meet its pension liabilities.[10] Already near the end of 2007, when RPF's funding ratio was at an ample 160%, the fund started to imple-ment a strategic hedge in order to protect its required coverage ratio from sharp drops in stock markets on the one hand and declines in interest rates on the other hand.[11] And exactly these market developments plunged many pension funds into trouble over 2008 and early 2009. RPF's measures made use of advanced option techniques, such as equity-linked receiver swaptions and put options on stocks that create a cover for sizeable falls in equity prices as well as in interest rates.

The strategic hedge directed the RPF to a funding ratio of 128.6% at the end of 2008, which is in view of the stormy financial weather a healthy number, especially when comparing this figure to that of other pension funds. In this way, RPF's policy protected its sponsor company from having to make extra contributions to the fund. Moreover RPF is among the few pension funds that could provide full indexation for its scheme members over 2009.[12]

Bernard Walschots, CIO at Dutch Rabobank Pension Fund, commented: "Because of the rising funding ratio (over 2007), we had the means to implement that strategic hedge. And of course, umbrellas are cheap when it is not raining".[13] However, the implementation of the hedging measures did cost Rabobank Pension Fund a considerable part of its return over 2007: 3.1% of the total return of 4.8%.[14] Obviously, RPF abandoned a part of the upward potential, "but the final result has made up for it."[15]

On the contrary, the Shell Pension Fund keeps open the upward potential of its funding ratio, but as a consequence the downward potential as well. Shell takes a different view on risk management, as the fund aims to achieve maximum investment results to maintain a healthy position over the long term.

In line with expectations, Shell invests 70% of its assets in equity-like products, including a considerable portion in emerging markets. Over the past years this combination has yielded above average returns,[16] which led to funding ratios of well over 180%[17] at the end of 2007 and in addition, to sharp drops in contributions from the sponsor Shell and its employees. However, this party ended abruptly in 2008 when Shell held on to its investment principles while stock markets collapsed: the funding ratio sunk to 85%, and as readily as they were cut back, the contributions have been put up again.

Although Shell Pension Fund has reduced its allocation towards equity as of the end of 2008, it sticks to its vision on managing risks. "We remain convinced that a pension fund must set its sight on the long term. You must continue to take a certain level of risk as you will otherwise not earn enough. Good returns are needed to meet pension commitments and if possible to apply indexation."[18]

10.2 Theory

Many argue that the world has become a riskier place. Politicians would single out 9/11. Economists would probably point to the interdependency of economies that provided no safe haven during the credit crisis of 2008. Investors would also suggest that the increasing volatility of securities markets makes them a more dangerous place to invest in. Safe havens are steadily disappearing; problems to finance government debt in Greece spiraled into a European debt crisis in just a few months in 2010, leaving investors to wonder which safe asset might be exposed next.

More asset managers than pension funds (8% versus 4%, see Table 14.1) formulate beliefs on *risk management*. Although risk as a separate belief is embedded in the financial market beliefs in the form of the risk-return relationship, risk management addresses a broader area than the assets themselves, including the implementation and monitoring of the investment process. Risk diversification is usually stressed as one of the key elements, especially by pension funds. Risk diversification reflects the trustee's interpretation of a "prudent person principle".

Table 10.1   Illustration of risk management investment beliefs

---

The board of trustees of the Local Authorities Pensions Plan (LAPP) states in its investment beliefs that: "The investment program will include a disciplined risk management approach which emphasizes diversification of assets and incorporates ongoing risk measurement and management, including risk budgeting."[19]

OMERS – Statement of Investment Beliefs. The investment organization should be efficient, innovative and allow for effective and timely decision-making. An effective investment operation with the appropriate culture will reduce the risk of unacceptable investment activities and behaviour.[20]

Ontario Teachers' Pension Plan believes that "the core building blocks underpinning our approach to risk management include the asset-mix policy, diversification within asset classes, risk budgeting, and ongoing monitoring to ensure we remain within our risk parameters. The policy of broad diversification across various asset classes is one of our most important risk management and control tools.[21]

Risk management is the reaction to risk by investors and pension funds as they attempt to ensure that the risks to which they are really exposed are the risks to which they think they are exposed and want to be exposed. Risk is a concept, and a business decision. Before developing a framework for managing risks responsibly, three basic fallacies should be avoided (Culp 2001):

- *Risk is always bad.* The common attitude toward risk is to consider it as a threat. In itself, risk is however neither a threat nor an opportunity. It simply exists. Culp illustrates this by bringing onstage the homeowner in South Carolina, for whom a hurricane represents a large risk. The supplier of sandbags and weather radios clearly sees it differently. For insurers, the hurricane presents a potentially insurable event; for the institutional investor buying catastrophe bonds, it presents a genuine risk diversification opportunity.

- *Some risks are so bad that they must be eliminated at all costs.* Rather, the reverse is true: there is *no* risk so great that it must be eliminated at all costs. Culp drives home two messages. First, risks must be eva-luated in terms of possible occurrence, not only in terms of consequences. Second, risks are about costs and benefits. A pension fund can fully hedge its inflation risk, but also part of it, weighing costs of unexpected inflation against the benefits of lower insurance. In other words, risks must be managed, not eliminated.
- *"Playing it safe" is really the safest thing to do.* Trustees and investors are also human, and prone to knee-jerk behavioral reactions. Which investor has not considered a radical switch from equities to bonds when the stock markets took a severe hit? However, this risk-averse behavior, though appearing safe, might have worse consequences in the long term.

Risk management should above all be a reflection of the true risks that a fund takes. Unfortunately, it takes a financial crisis to expose all the (un)expected risks that a fund takes, before a proper assessment can be made which ones need to be shed, and which one need to be managed and focused on. The pension deal is crucial here. To put it bluntly, participants in a Collective Defined Contribution (CDC) scheme should be more interested in a high and stable return, since their pension rights are more dependent on capital accumulation than with Defined Benefit schemes. Identifying the risks that really matter leads to different strategic views. There are three major risks faced by a pension plan (Muralidhar and Asad-Syed 2001):

- The asset-liability risk, or the risk that occurs when the board selects a benchmark which imperfectly emulates the liability.
- The tactical or benchmark risk taken by internal staff or external managers (such as tactical asset allocation, the over- or underweighting of asset classes and countries, or investment styles such as capitalization segments) with the purpose of adding value over the investment benchmark.

- The active risk taken by investment managers, who are overseen by internal staff, in an attempt to add value relative to the indices against which they are measured.

There are many types of risks in the financial sphere. The asset manager is happy to point out that each one should be considered by the pension plan. However, given the three major sources of risk described earlier, it makes sense for a fund to develop beliefs about the trade-off between managing risks as a fund, and the rewards of risks. Basically, two strategic choices emerge:

- *Manageable and rewarding risks.* Risks like the equity risk and illiquidity risk fall into this category. The equity risk premium is the long-term expected difference between the return on risky stocks and the return on safe bonds, and is one of the major choices and risks pension funds have to manage. Pension funds can also choose to earn an illiquidity premium on their investments: an additional return for strategies of holding assets that are bought and sold in illiquid markets.
- *Unmanageable and non-rewarding risks.* Risks like interest rate and currency fall into this category. For pension funds, the value of the liabilities depends on the level of interest rates. Small changes in interest rates might have large consequences in valuation of liabilities; a decreasing interest rate in combination with decreasing securities prices in particular has adverse consequence for the solvency of pension funds. This interest rate risk is typically too large to manage, which is the main reason why funds tend to hedge it. Funds incur currency risk because part of the risk-spreading strategy involves investing in foreign currencies, while the pension liabilities are paid in home currency. This is a strategic reason for currency risk. Operationally, the foreign currency market is considered to be one of the most liquid markets. In the long term, currencies earn little return but generate disproportionally large risks.

We stress the combination of manageability and reward. If risks seem rewarding, but the governance to manage it is feeble, risks easily overtake potential rewards. The choice between these two strategic types of risk also depends on the governance of the fund. For example, active risk – risk allocated to managers or strategies with an active investment style – has many hurdles to success: identifying inefficiencies, building a consistent investment philosophy and process, and executing it diligently. Funds with better governance and resources to manage and monitor this might well consider this a manageable and rewarding risk. The size of the fund is not the issue here, it's the investment committee, playing a crucial role in determining this trade-off.

Typically, the investment committee responsible for setting the strategic asset allocation of the fund also sets the overall risk budget, deciding how it wants to allocate risks among asset classes or (active) managers to achieve the highest risk-adjusted return (Berkelaar et al. 2006). Risk budgeting involves and uses risk measurement, risk attribution and risk allocation. After deciding the strategic asset allocation, institutional investors generally allocate risk to three active investment decisions: tactical asset allocation among asset classes (e.g. market timing between stocks and bonds), tactical asset allocation within asset classes (e.g. growth versus value) and manager/security selection. These activities have different risk and return characteristics.

The bias in measuring risks for pension funds tends to be towards relative risk measures, risks relative to benchmarks, rather than absolute risk measures.

Each of these three categories can be further subdivided – by interest rate risk, equity risk, inflation risk, etc. One of the major advances in recent years is Liability-Driven Investments (LDI), developed to put risk firmly at the heart of investment management. This is a strategic framework for mapping and managing liabilities. LDI rejects the traditional model for asset allocation that revolves around the split between equities and bonds. Performance is no longer measured against a market index whose constituents may not have any relevance to a particular scheme. Each scheme has its own risk profile and patterns of liability. It is a scheme's ability to meet these commitments that determines its approach to risk. The two key rates that have far-reaching implications for the extent of a scheme's liability are interest and inflation rates. Essentially, LDI is about isolating these risks and nullifying their effect (Ellison and Jolly 2009). Other crucial assumptions are about whether mortality will rise, and whether the sponsoring company will fail.

10.3   Debates to be aware of

Trustees should clearly formulate the focal point of the pension fund's risk management, especially when the assets are managed outside the pension fund, which is the case with many funds. The incentive for the manager of the external mandate is outperformance relative to the benchmark; all the mandates together do not add up to the total return/risk goals of the fund. Consider for example two securities A and B.[22] Security A has an expected return in line with the market and a relatively lower risk than the market. Security B on the other hand has a higher expected return than the market, but with considerably more risk. Chances are that the external manager opts for B, as it increases his chances of outperformance and a performance fee, whereas the fund would be better off with Security A.

Koijen et al. (2008) identify three problems when awarding external mandates. The first is a technical one. Some diversification is lost when funds first optimize asset allocation and then select the best managers and investment strategies within the asset allocation mix, instead of optimizing the portfolio directly in relation to the existing strategies. A second, subtler issue is the principal–agent issue. There may be considerable, but unobservable, differences in appetites for risk between the pension fund and each of the asset managers. When the fund only knows how the risk appetite is distributed among the investment managers, but does not know what appetite for risk the individual manager has, delegating portfolio decisions to multiple managers might turn out to be costly. A third issue is investment horizon. Pension funds have a long investment horizon, while the managers are usually compensated on an annual basis.

Risk management's finest hours should be in financial crises. Crises are embedded within our financial system and therefore part of risk management. We should not reason them away, but should exercise and train for their regular occurrence, in the same way as fireman and ambulance staff train for the emergencies they deal with. Crisis is part and parcel of a cycle of financial innovation and restructuring. Risk managers should not however confuse the theoretical chance of severe volatility and turbulence in the financial markets with the actual occurrence. Volatility in financial markets has been steadily increasing since the 1970s – say since the collapse of Bretton Woods in 1971 – and risk modeling has been systematically lagging behind. This has everything to do with a dramatic shift in the business model of financial services companies, from rather dull interest income to more exciting fee income, which is highly dependent on the direction and activity of the financial markets. We should not forget ordinary commercial companies here, with their treasury activities, leasing etc. They play their part as well. And banks have more or less "taken on board" the volatility of the financial markets, thereby themselves increasing the inherent instability in financial markets. This long-term structural increase implies that risk simply always lags behind – models do not see this megatrend, they just reflect what the risk would be in the previous crisis. So yes it is indeed extreme, but it is not entirely unexpected.

It pays to know what you are asking in risk management, and who you are asking. Yet you only know what to ask if you know what is important. Pension funds generally apply sophisticated risk models, and trustees are informed on a regular basis on the probability of the fund slipping below the minimum required cover ratio of 105% – that is where the real problems for trustees start. A typical reaction among trustees in 2008 was: How on earth is it possible that we moved from a cover ratio of 150 a year ago to below 105 now? Why did we not buy insurance beforehand? And the answer is as follows: at 150 the probability of nose-diving under 105 was negligible. Probability is however a miserable guide. We could blame the risk model, but that is unfair. It pays to know what you are asking in risk management.

Besides knowing what to ask in risk management, it also pays to know who the stakeholders are in risk management. There may be underlying or additional beliefs that have to be made explicit – the emotional loss-aversion characteristic of trustees, alongside the rational loss-avoiding function of a pension fund embodied in Asset-Liability Modeling (ALM).

Kritzman (2002) provides a pleasantly confusing example of how loss depends on how you frame the question. Suppose that the investment committee has to decide on the strategic asset allocation, and the following information is known: the expected average yearly return is 10%, and the standard deviation, 20%. How safe is the portfolio? Based on the information, Kritzman serves up five variants for calculating the likelihood of loss:

- Likelihood single year loss: 14%
- Likelihood average annual loss: 0.03%
- Likelihood cumulative loss: 3%
- Likelihood loss in >1 years: 77%
- Likelihood cumulative loss at some point: 54%

Which number will you use in a discussion with trustees?

Trustees increasingly feel that they are at a loss to know what to do right now. On the other hand, they were given all the information, in neat tables with percentages. These percentages do not prepare them for an extreme situation like today. Trustees should not work with abstract figures alone, but should be trained to cope with real live situations (especially the bad ones). What will your actions be when the cover ratio is 150% : 105% : 90%? How will stakeholders react? Will you still rebalance or not? These are kind of situations trustees should get familiar with. This type of training will help a fund cope with future crises, and is especially helpful in an unstable environment where the time span between the occurrence of financial and economic crises continually decreases (cf. Reinhart and Rogoff 2009). Preparation and training is no news for large funds with dynamic ALM, but an innovation for smaller funds. We expect firemen and ambulances to practice regularly for unexpected situations, so why not the trustees to whom I have delegated the task of providing for my income once I am 65, the prospective pensioner could justifiably ask.

At the risk of stating the obvious, risk management runs the "risk" of over-quantification, where spuriously precise models and measurement obscure the meaning of risk management. For example, take an investment objective formulated as: "to produce a negative return in no more than 1 year in 10". If a manager produces negative returns in two consecutive years, most investors would conclude that the manager has failed to meet the objective. But this is not the case. Statistics show that the investor would need about 100 years to be 90% sure that the manager failed to meet the objective. This is too long for most risk managers. So the alternative is to split up years in quarters, and repeat the exercise. However, noise then gets in the way. Thus although the objective appears both rational and measurable, measurement dominates meaning (Gray 1997).

11
Investment Style

Summary

✓ Investment styles are the approaches investment managers take to investing; a consistent investment style can be traced back to inefficiencies in the financial markets.

✓ The number of basic investment styles is limited, despite the large diversity of strategies based on it.

✓ Value versus growth, small cap vs. large cap, or top down vs. bottom up are classic choices.

✓ New investment styles and strategies are tricky: they appeal to the innovative side of investors. You have to ask yourselves whether you are willing to go with a new investment style that has not yet been tested and proven, and whether your governance is up to it.

11.1 Case study

How do you hold on to your investment style when things are getting ugly for your company in terms of performance? Brandes Investment Partners, managing $42 billion in value-oriented strategies for their clients, has been down this road many times since its founding in 1974.[1]

Value investing is a "classic" in the investment industry, and can be traced back to the investment principles of Ben Graham and David Dodd. The basic idea is to select securities that trade at a market price that is less than their intrinsic value. Since securities do not have one "correct" intrinsic value, it is vitally important to develop valuation methods and to maintain a so-called "margin of safety" with respect to the intrinsic value when buying undervalued stocks. Value investors believe that in the long run, the market price of an undervalued security will return to its intrinsic value, so that investing in undervalued securities pays off. Established in San Diego, Brandes Investment Partners is an asset management company that has built its investment philosophy firmly on the principles of value investing:

> We consistently apply the value investing philosophy in all market con-ditions – and to every portfolio we manage. We firmly believe invest-ment success is driven by the identification and purchase of securities trading at discounts to their intrinsic value estimates. In our opinion, the benefits of this approach are evident in the long-term results we have achieved.[2]

In the early 1970s, young Charles Brandes met Ben Graham, one of the fathers of value investing. Inspired by Graham's ideas, and armed with what he believed was a proven methodology for evaluating businesses, Brandes completely embraced the "value philosophy".[3] After the bear market of 1973–1974, Brandes observed that many stocks were extremely undervalued and in line with the value philosophy, he decided that this was the right time to start his own investment firm.[4] Since 1974 Brandes Investment has become one of the leading value-based asset management companies and at the end of 2007 the company was managing assets of over $111.6 billion.[5]

However, as Brandes itself also recognizes, sticking to an investment style might pay off in the long term but runs the danger of being in and out of favor with investors, possibly for long periods. In 2006, it went through a challenging period[6] and the first half of 2008 proved to be no better for Brandes Investment Partners. The San Diego firm's assets dropped 23% in six months and it was heavily underperforming several benchmarks. For Indiana Public Employees' Retirement Fund and San Francisco City & County Employees' Retirement System, both clients of Brandes, this was sufficient reason to (partially) drop Brandes Investment.[7] By the end of 2008, Brandes only had $52.9 billion worth of assets under management.[8] "Yes, they have underperformed, but we are not surprised. The markets have not favored Brandes' approach", said H. Craig Slaughter of Virginia Investment Management Board, another client of Brandes Investment, commenting on its performance.[9]

How can Brandes nevertheless stick to its style? While some major asset managers like UBS have already bid farewell to the value-based strategy, Brandes imperturbably stays faithful to it. It has its reasons. First, Brandes points to its more than 35 years of experience in value investing as proof that the firm possesses the competencies needed to survive as value investor. Second, Brandes believes that its time as value investor is yet to come again: "When the principles of value investing are applied, perhaps the most fortuitous time for value investors is when pessimism has been rampant and, as we believe today, indiscriminate."[10] Charles Brandes also keeps his eye firmly on the long run: "I am not concerned with our recent under-performance (..). We believe that our portfolios are currently well-positioned for long-term appreciation."[11]

But perhaps the key success factor for sticking to an investment style is communication. At the end of the day, Brandes' investment philosophy is very clear and since Brandes has strong communication with its clients, they know what to expect of its approach. Clients that stick to Brandes not only choose to invest according to its investment belief, but also share the theory and argumentation behind it.

11.2   Theory

Investment managers usually describe their activities as having a "style" that describes their approach to investing. Investment style refers to the approach they use in selecting individual investments and creating port-folios to achieve their investment goals.[12] For example, a fund that special-izes in small-cap equities might seek long-term capital appreciation by choosing aggressive growth stocks. Another small-cap fund with the same objective might build a portfolio of underpriced value stocks. Evaluating a fund's investment style is an important consideration in determining the added value of an investor. Styles can be subjective and change as their markets change.

Another investment style could simply be to avoid dominant invest-ment styles. Knut Kjaer, executive director at the Norwegian Government Pension fund, says its approach is to avoid overarching, top-down strategic investment directives and instead rely on a large number of individual and mutually independent investment decisions.[13]

Pension funds and asset managers adhere to a wide range of investment styles; Table 11.1 lists the most common known today. Both pension funds (16%) and asset managers (17%) explicitly formulate their investment man-agement styles. For pension funds, 5% of their beliefs deal with the classic active-passive management style.

Table 11.1   Investment styles

Investment style	Underlying belief
Active vs. passive	Markets where inefficiencies do exist and can be exploited (active) versus market inefficiencies do not exist and cannot be exploited, or market inefficiencies do exist but the costs and uncertainties of exploiting them are too high in relation the expected returns (passive).
Index styles	The current indices do not reflect the markets adequately. Alternatives are sought in "fundamental" indexing, or variants like wealth weighted or cap weighted indices.
Value vs. growth	Investors overreact in the short term in overpricing fast-growing companies (growth stocks) relative to slow growth companies (value stocks).
Large vs. small cap	Large caps are priced more efficiently due to high coverage; information advantage does not pay off. Companies with a small market capitalization on the other hand are less well covered by analysts, therefore it pays to build up an information advantage and base a strategy on it.
Absolute return	Strategies based on the risk of loss or underperforming cash, rather than underperforming a market index.
Relative return	Strategies based on the evaluation and performance of benchmarks, with the aim of at least replicating the benchmark risk and return (index tracking) or exceeding it (enhanced index, active management).
Minimum variance	Target returns can be achieved with lower levels of risk than predictedby the Efficient Market Hypothesis.
Behavioral finance styles	Strategies that exploit psychology-related biases and tendencies, causing investors to behave irrationally.
Top-down vs. bottom-up	Identifying investment options by analyzing market trends (top-down) vs. identifying investment options by analyzing individual stocks showing good performances (bottom-up).
Liquid vs. illiquid	Investments that can easily be converted back into cash with a minimum loss of price (liquid) versus investments that are hard to sell at a price close to market value, for which risk investors require additional returns.
Contrarian	Investing in a manner that differs from the conventional wisdom, when the consensus opinion appears to be wrong from the viewpoint of the investor.
Benchmark free investing	Holding a portfolio, free of a benchmark, which might generate a higher absolute return, but adds more volatility and uncertainty.

11.2.1 Active vs. passive

With passive management, portfolio managers bet on the movement of entire markets, for financial as well as real assets, assuming that these markets are efficiently priced. With active management selection, the focus is on picking good investments within each market. A belief in inefficiencies in the pricing of markets can well be combined with a belief in the efficiency of pricing individual securities in that market, and vice versa. Additionally, efficiencies might exist in the short term but disappear in the long term and vice versa.

The delineation between passive and active management can be directly traced back to the efficient markets hypothesis (EMH), theorizing that all available information is embedded in the pricing of the security. However, nuances matter. The EMH is interpreted by some to mean "asset prices are 'correct' at any given point in time" (cf. Shiller 2003), while others interpret it as "markets not allowing investors to earn above-average returns without accepting above-average risks" (Malkiel 2003).

Not all funds adhere to an active management style. Active management is more costly than a passive indexing strategy, and it may not generate higher net returns after management fees (Mitchell and Hsin 1997a; Mitchell and Hsin 1997b). The core-satellite concept combines a passive style in efficient markets with an active style in less efficient markets.

The active-passive debate is especially relevant for liquid markets, like bonds, equities, listed real estate and commodities. In more specialized illiquid markets, like unlisted real estate, investors have no opportunity to emulate entire markets. Particularly since the 1990s, the share of passively managed assets has increased substantially, for example from 11% in 2003 to 16% in 2007 for the US market.[14] While the increase is striking, the real question here is why 75% or 80% of pension fund assets are not passively managed.

11.2.2 Index styles

An alternative for finding new ways of earning excess returns relative to the index benchmark is to try to create benchmarks with superior returns. Fundamental indexing appeared on the scene in 2005 when Arnott et al. (2005) introduced this as a superior alternative to the traditional approach of indexing the market by constructing capitalization-weighted portfolios.

Normally, an index is constructed by constructing a portfolio of securities where the relative weight reflects the market capitalization. The main idea behind this is that markets are efficient – the market value of a security includes all available information about the company's prospects, so an index that accurately represents a market should do likewise.

Fundamental indexing is however based on other weighting measures like earnings or dividends. The reasoning reflects a different belief: suppose markets are not efficient, then there are bound to be overvalued and undervalued companies. In an index, the overvalued companies will carry relatively more weight (they are after all overvalued) to the undervalued. Therefore, its performance will be relatively depressed compared with an index that does not overweight overvalued companies. No investor doubts that there are overvalued companies in an index; it is simply extremely hard to identify them. While simulations show good results with fundamental indices, critics justifiably retort that this is just a smart form of investment style, like small versus large cap and value versus growth, since fundamental indices tend to overweigh smaller companies and value companies (McQuarrie 2008).

11.2.3   Value versus growth

Active investors can be divided into growth and value seekers. Proponents of growth seek companies they expect (on average) to increase earnings by 15% to 25%. Value investors look for bargains – cheap stocks that are often out of favor, such as cyclical stocks at the low end of their business cycle. A value investor primarily selects asset-oriented stocks with low prices compared to underlying book, replacement, or liquidation values (Rao 2007). Together, the two categories can also provide a diversification effect: returns on growth stocks and value stocks are not highly correlated. By diversifying between growth and value, investors can help manage risk.

Value strategies are suited to a long time horizon – cheap stocks need to be given time to recover in value (Haugen 2003). Long periods – possibly stretching decades – seriously test the determination of investors – how long are you willing to stick to your belief? In the 1990s, UBS Asset Management did its homework too and decided that institutional investors were best served by a value approach. It changed its investment process in a global overhaul. Clients however became increasingly disgruntled in the late 1990s when they saw the gap between growth and value stocks increase dramatically. Growth stocks in the late 1990s meant investing in internet and telecom ("dot.com") companies, with spectacular IPOs and investor returns.[15] Clients increasingly defected from UBS. Faced with the loss of yet more clients, UBS abandoned its approach and appeared to move towards more growth stocks. The rest is history. Stock markets fell by almost 50% in two years, driven by the fall in growth stocks, and a value approach would have fared far better. To avoid such issues in the future, an effective approach is taken by Dutch healthcare pension fund PFZW: allocate part of the strategic portfolio to value stocks and measure it against an appropriate value benchmark – the long-term horizon needed to capitalize on value stocks is internalized.

11.2.4 Large versus small cap

Some investors use the size of a company as the basis for investing. Studies of stock returns going back to 1925 have suggested that "smaller is better." On average, the highest returns have come from stocks with the lowest market capitalization (common shares outstanding times share price). But since these returns tend to run in cycles, there have been long periods when large-cap stocks have outperformed smaller stocks. Also, at an early stage, small-cap stocks had bigger premiums and were more expensive to buy and sell, but this is not easily captured in historical analysis, and in reality likely skewed total return for investors. Small-cap stocks also have higher price volatility, which translates into higher risk.

Table 11.2   Illustration of investment management style investment beliefs

---

For Dutch civil servants' pension fund ABP, "Valuations revert to a mean over a longer period."[16]

Danish Pensioninsurer PensionDanmark "take well-considered investment decisions based on long-term thinking and valuation. By nature our investment style is contrarian and value orientated."[17]

11.2.5 Absolute returns

Absolute return strategies aim to produce a positive absolute return in euros or dollars, regardless of the direction of financial markets. As an investment vehicle, an absolute return fund seeks to achieve positive returns by employing investment management techniques that differ from traditional ones. Absolute return investment techniques include using short selling, futures, options, derivatives, arbitrage, leverage and unconventional assets. The key idea behind absolute return investment is to compile a portfolio with a low correlation with financial market performance. Alfred Winslow Jones is credited with being the first compiler of an absolute return fund, in 1949. The prevalence of this type of fund has grown significantly in the past decades and these funds are presently mainly known as "hedge funds".

11.2.6   Relative returns

For most investors and fund, relative return strategies take up most of the implementation of the portfolio. While absolute return strategies are concerned with the return of a particular asset and do not use benchmarks, relative return strategies are based on the evaluation and performance of benchmarks. This means that when a relative return strategy is in place, a fund manager will compare its performance to the benchmark, and adjust its portfolio to "beat" the benchmark, creating excess returns, after costs and after correcting for any additional market risk taken. If the fund is underperforming, the manager will evaluate the fund's strategy in relation to the benchmark strategy and adjust its strategy accordingly.

11.2.7   Minimum variance

Interest in minimum variance portfolios was initiated by Robert Haugen, who claimed that a portfolio designed to minimize total risk achieved an absolute return, as well as risk-adjusted return, above its benchmark. The minimum-variance portfolio is interesting because it does not require expected asset returns, but only the correlation between assets, which is more stable (Behr et al. 2008). Researchers have estimated the performance of this portfolio and compared it to other portfolios; some found that this portfolio outperforms a value-weighted portfolio (Baker and Haugen 1991; Clarke and Thorley 2006).

This flies in the face of the efficient market hypothesis, stating that it is impossible to consistently outperform the market by using any information that the market already knows. Minimum variance strategies tend to outperform in relative terms in bear markets, but can underperform in thematically-driven bull markets, such as the technology bubble. Even the minimum variance can be beaten in terms of performance and Sharpe ratios, by equally weighting every stock in a given universe.[18]

11.2.8   Behavioral finance styles

Behavioral Finance has attracted a lot of attention in academia in the last 20 years, and has enriched the vocabulary of investors with terms like herding, overreaction, myopia and loss aversion. In recent years it has started to evolve into an investment style. Behavioral finance tries to explain market anomalies, offering the potential for positive excess returns, by positing that psychology-related biases and tendencies cause investors to act irrationally, which leads to systematic mispricing of assets – which is maintained for a period. This implies opportunities for excess returns for an investor who understands the source of the systematic mispricing and can overcome the obstacle to arbitrage (Wright et al. 2008). In a sense, most investment styles are behavioral finance related – small versus large cap, or value versus growth, imply systematic mispricing that we are rationally aware of. Investors however face serious obstacles to exploiting this – for example, the time horizon needed to earn excess returns.

11.2.9   Top-down versus bottom-up

There has been much debate on the top-down and bottom-up approaches to investing, yet relatively little research has been done to evaluate its merits. With the top-down approach, investors study the economic trends and then determine the industries and companies that are likely to benefit the most from them. Top-down investors will first look at the entire market as well as the economy, and try to identify the main market trend ahead of other players. They believe that picking individual companies comes second because if the economic conditions are not right for the industry that a company operates in, it will be difficult for the company to generate profits, regardless of how efficient it is. Negative events, like high interest and inflation rates or currency depreciation, can affect a country's economy and cause stock prices to tumble. Predicting how currencies and interest rates move determines the subsequent asset allocation. Taking this one step further, it can also determine sector allocation: for example, interest rate movements hit the valuation of banks in a different way than that of airlines. However, such investors may sometimes miss good companies that are still performing well, even in a depressed sector.

On the other hand, famous investment experts like Warren Buffet, managing the $261 billion Berkshire Hathaway Fund,[19] and Peter Lynch, best-known for managing Fidelity Investment's largest funds, favor the bottom-up approach. They say that macro-economic forecasts are actually major distractions for investors as the projections might turn out to be wrong. Instead, investors' efforts should concentrate more on detecting the quality of earnings and asset value of the individual company. Bottom-up investors therefore conduct extensive research on individual companies. As long as the company's future prospects look strong, the economic, market or industry cycles are of no concern. In fact, a downturn in the stock market may provide investors with a good margin of safety for buying stocks at depressed levels and riding them up to big gains. So, bottom-up managers will buy stocks even though the macro-economic and industry outlooks appear uncertain. When the industry may be out of favor and most investors are ignoring the true earnings of companies, bottom-up managers can detect good and well-managed ones selling at prices that are far lower than their intrinsic value.[20] However, bottom-up managers may sometimes fail to see the wood for the trees. They may identify certain companies but miss the overall industry trend. This is especially a risk for theme funds, where managers are bound by the mandate to start or to keep investing in a specific sector.

The top-down and bottom-up approaches are two distinct and fundamentally very different approaches to investing. Investors can combine the top-down and bottom-up approaches by applying top-down analysis to asset allocation decisions while using a bottom-up approach to selecting the individual securities in the portfolio.

11.2.10 Liquid versus illiquid

Whereas liquid investments can be considered relatively safe as they can be converted into cash quickly with a minimum risk of price erosion, illiquid investments are more risky as they are harder to buy or sell quickly enough to prevent or minimize value reduction. Hence, making illiquid investments means you are running the liquidity risk – the risk stemming from the lack of marketability of your investment – and investors expect to be rewarded for this in terms of additional return. The liquidity risk is particularly significant during volatile periods. NBER (National Bureau of Economic Research 2009) mentions on its website: "If [investors] evaluate illiquid assets based on their average risk ..., failing to note that they can become considerably riskier during volatile times, then investment strategies could appear better than they actually are."[21]

11.2.11 Contrarian

A contrarian is one who invests in a manner that differs from the conventional wisdom. It is an investment style that goes against prevailing market trends as investments are made in poorly performing assets. The aim of the contrarian is to sell these assets again when they perform well. The underlying belief of the contrarian investor is that certain crowd behavior among investors will influence the price of assets in a way that does not reflect their true value. For example, when pessimism about a certain stock prevails, its price can be driven down so low that this overstates the company's risks and understates its prospects. Investing in this stock might yield above-average returns. On the other hand, widespread optimism may result in overvaluation. Hence, a contrarian is most likely to avoid extremely booming markets. Warren Buffet stands out as one of the world's most famous contrarians. One of his favorite sayings is that "you should be fearful when others are greedy, and be greedy when others are fearful."[22]

11.2.12   Benchmark-free investing

This investment style, basically a variant of absolute return investing, targets high absolute returns without references to a benchmark, while accepting potentially higher item volatility. The main idea is that market benchmarks discourage managers from holding investments outside the benchmark universe and encourage them to hold investments they do not like solely for risk control purpose. Also, benchmarks do little to protect investments in bear markets (Watson Wyatt Worldwide 2005). Lifting benchmark restrictions however assumes that a sub-group of skilled investors will surface, defying adverse market conditions, and moreover, that trustees and their advisors have the selection skills to identify these managers. Waring and Siegel (2006) argue that benchmark-free investing is more a matter of not being clear what the benchmark should be than actually an investment style.

11.3   Debates to be aware of

Investment styles basically do not differ that much from normal product offerings. If you are buying a product that was introduced 20 years ago, chances are that most of the bugs are out of the product, and that you pretty much know what you are buying into. Value versus growth, small cap versus large cap, or top-down versus bottom-up are such classic choices. You would not be praised for your innovative and daring choices, rather your steadfastness in sticking to tradition. On the other hand, if you crave to be an early adaptor or innovator, benchmark-free investing, absolute return or fundamental indexing should attract your attention. The attraction is rational – earning excess returns by being one of the first to enter these new markets – but also psychological – upholding an image as innovator and pro-active investor. However, as the recent turmoil in the financial markets has shown, an innovator has to be aware of what he is buying into. New innovative investments like hedge funds have only recently started to go "full circle", giving the investment industry insights into the downside as well as the upside potential of the strategies.

Academic debate has been driving the changes in investment styles. Managers can shift their investment style when market conditions change as shown in Figure 11.1. For example, passive management took off once investors became increasingly disappointed with the results of active management.

Figure 11.1   Developments in investment styles

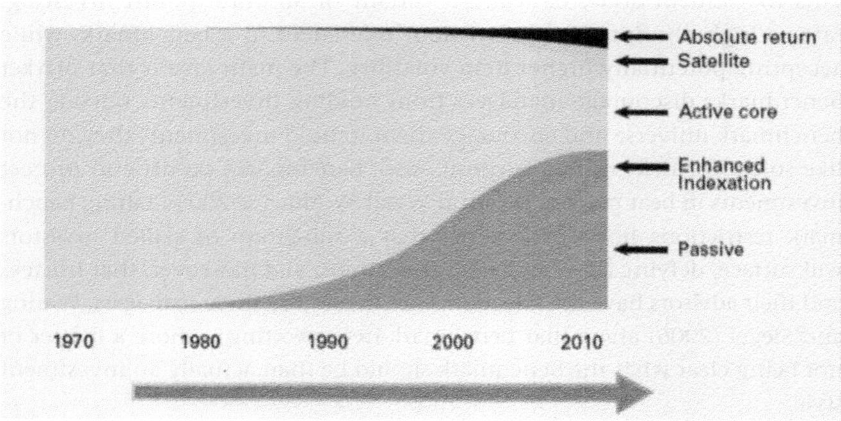

Source: Watson Wyatt Worldwide (2005)

The investment style has implications for the organization. An organization with a bottom-up approach needs analysts or access to analyst skills; a top-down organization needs investment strategists for portfolio construction. Since the bottom-up approach is more labor intensive than the top-down approach, organizations with a small staff and overhead, like many pension funds, tend to favor the top-down approach.

12
Costs

Summary

✓ Beliefs about costs are based on the premise that, all other things being equal, lower investment costs are always better than higher ones.

✓ Asset managers aim to convince clients that the net return matters, not the costs. This sounds nice in theory, but does not quite work out in the same way in practice. Costs are certain, expected returns are not.

✓ Higher costs may point to something undesirable for trustees, called agency costs. To reduce these costs, an efficient compensation structure should be designed to better align the interests of the trustee and the asset manager.

12.1 Case study

"To pay no attention to costs is probably the biggest dumb mistake investors can make."[1] The words strike home from the mouth of John ("Jack") Bogle, a veteran in the investment industry, widely known as the founder of one trillion dollar asset management firm Vanguard Group. He estimates that total costs in 2007 amounted to $528 billion in the US alone (Bogle 2008). Bogle knows better than anyone else the long-term impact of fees, commissions, taxes and other kind of costs on the net return of investments, advertising this as "the Magic of Compounding vs. the Tyranny of Compounding Costs":[2] the "magical" impact of combining a reasonable rate of return with the concept of time alone, versus the adverse effect that costs have on this process.

To illustrate this, consider the following simple example. Over the past 20 years, a simple, low-cost stock market index fund produced an annual return of 12.8% – just below the 13% return of the market itself. During the same period, the average equity mutual fund delivered – largely due to investment costs – a return of just 10%, a shortfall compared with the index fund of 2.8% per year. Compounded over that period, each dollar invested in the low-cost index fund grew to $11.1, while $1 invested in the average equity fund grew to just $6.7[3] (see Figure 12.1).

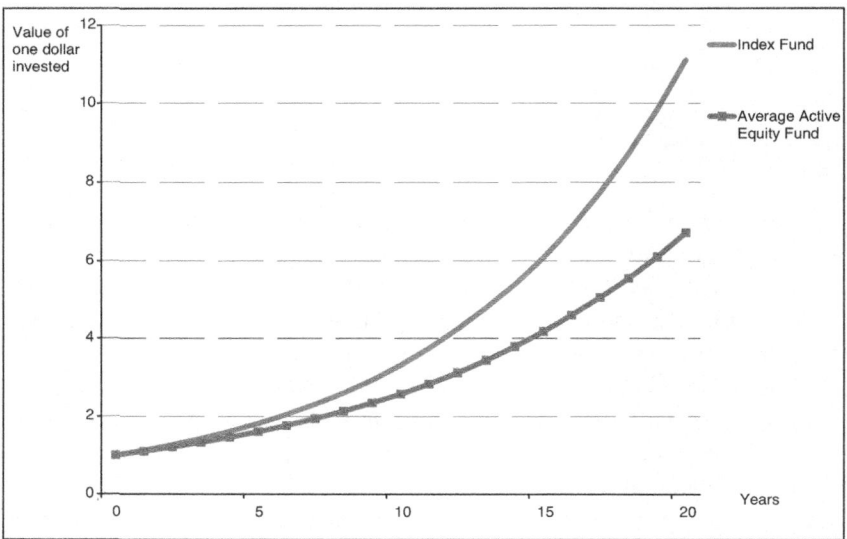

Figure 12.1   The magic of compounding vs. the tyranny of compounding costs

Although the impact of costs comes down to simple arithmetic, it seems that Bogle's urgent message of cost awareness has not yet fully penetrated the investment business.[4] For pension funds, things appear to be somewhat brighter, but they too have much room for improvement, as there still seems to be a large range of administrative and investment costs across pension funds[5] (cf. Bikker and De Dreu 2007).

Founded in 1974, John Bogle's Vanguard Group is one of the few asset managers with a very clear focus on minimizing costs for its investors. Vanguard's belief in efficient financial markets (see Chapter 5) combined with its "Costs matter" philosophy led in 1975 to the introduction of the first index fund.[6] Bogle: "If mutual funds as a group fail to deliver stock markets returns by the amount of their heavy costs, why not own the entire market at minimal costs?"[7] Instead of actively trying to earn excess returns in exchange for high manager fees, one simply tracks down the market index at low costs so that, even in case of outperformance, the after-costs investment return of the index funds still exceeds the return of the active strategy.

Initially, people in the business described it as a flawed concept, enticing investors to mediocrity. Why would an investor settle for average returns? It was even labeled as "Bogle's folly".[8] But eventually this "folly" paid off handsomely and by the start of 2009, $370 billion worth of assets were invested in Vanguard's index funds.

However, Vanguard is not low-cost just because it runs some index tracking funds. The average expense ratio for Vanguard's index trackers is 0.15% per year, against 0.89% for the average US index fund. Moreover Vanguard even manages active funds costing 0.26% a year compared with 1.25% for the average US mutual fund. Overall, Vanguard boasts a 1.02% annual cost advantage.[9] This is a major benefit, especially when one allows the 'Tyranny of compounding costs' to do its magic trick over time.

So far, Vanguard has yet to persuade major followers to adopt Bogle's line of thinking.[10] Worldwide, 84% remain invested in actively managed assets – old habits die hard.[11] Why is it that Vanguard remains one of the few in the vanguard of low-cost propaganda?

Probably, the words of writer Upton Sinclair hit the nail on the head: "It's amazing how difficult it is for a man to understand something if he's paid a small fortune not to understand it."[12] Or maybe it is Bogle's strong conviction and his never-ending struggle against the role of active managers who claim to add value on top of market returns while in many cases they actually erode value. But perhaps the most significant factor is the way Vanguard Group has created its structure to make its low-cost philosophy work. Vanguard is run as a mutually owned business. All the company's assets are owned by the funds that it manages for its investors.[13] It has no controlling shareholders extracting profits; all profits are reinvested into the fund management organization, seamlessly avoiding costly agency problems within the firm. Moreover, Vanguard achieves low costs by paying minimal commission to intermediaries, incurring minimal advertising costs and shaping its funds such that investor taxes are minimal.[14]

For the "poor" investor, these factors contribute to an approximate 1% cost advantage while providing a guarantee of net investment returns just shy of the market return. This creates a massive – if not impossible – challenge for active managers, who must outperform the market each and every year by at least 1% to provide investors with a higher net return than a low-cost index fund like Vanguard's. Applying "the relentless rules of simple arithmetic"[15] should be part of the investment curriculum.

12.2   Theory

Why should costs merit an investment belief? Beliefs about costs are based on the premise that, all other things being equal, lower investment costs are always better than higher investment costs. As economists – and John Bogle – like to say, all things being equal, higher costs lead to a lower net return. The investment professional will retort by pointing out that net return matters in the end, not the costs incurred. True, but the high cost base is a major factor explaining why mutual funds generally struggle to deliver higher than benchmark returns after costs.

Pension funds on the other hand have substantially lower costs, raising net returns, especially for large compulsory schemes. Low costs are a strategic "unique selling point" of pension funds, and are in some countries even considered as a license-to-operate, a major reason for pension funds to exist.[16] Commercial pension insurers regularly accuse compulsory pension schemes in Europe of unfair competition and market distortion, but the latter's low operating cost and higher net return usually tip the political debate in favor of pension funds.

Table 12.1   Illustration of costs investment beliefs

Vanguard believes that "minimizing the costs of investing is vital for long-term investment success."

Canadian Local Authorities Pension Plan LAPP also centers on costs, believing that "adopting different investment styles can reduce the potentially positive impact of active management, can increase the cost of managing the pension fund and can increase the time and cost of monitoring the investment management."

Average investment management fees paid by pension funds globally increased by 50% in five years to 110 basis points in 2007 from 65 basis points in 2002, according to a report published by Watson Wyatt in February 2008.[17] External active managers were responsible for the bulk of the increase.

Also on the negative side, higher costs may point to something undesirable for trustees called agency costs – costs that arise when an investment manager working on behalf of a pension fund is not fully motivated to help to achieve the funds' goals (see Figure 4.1).[18] Bauer and Frehen (2008) compared costs of pension funds and mutual funds and after correcting for differences in size, risk and other relevant factors, they still see a gap that is too large. Also, trustees assume that they are paying high fees to reward manager skills. A Watson Wyatt report (Smith 2008) asserted that this is not the case, attributing performance in recent years to the strength of markets and the use of leverage by managers to boost returns. Consultant Paul Trickett of Watson Wyatt warns that annual performance fees "amount to a free option for the manager, as the upside is uncapped but the downside is limited to the base fee."[19] Craig Baker, also from Watson Wyatt, urges funds to look carefully at whether they are paying for outperformance or for market returns. The downturn in financial markets – resulting from the financial crisis – provides ideal conditions for renegotiating fees, getting managers to charge a lower flat fee and a performance fee so that higher fees would only be paid for higher returns.[20] The combination of a high share of performance fees and low share of flat fees is considered the ideal combination to deal with the principal–agent model (Figure 12.2). Asset managers realize this; yet are reluctant to shift towards this model.

Reducing costs can be an investment belief based on economies of scale. A drive to avoid high-cost assets (such as private equity or hedge funds) or focus on low-cost strategies in large, liquid, efficient markets can constitute an alternative investment belief.

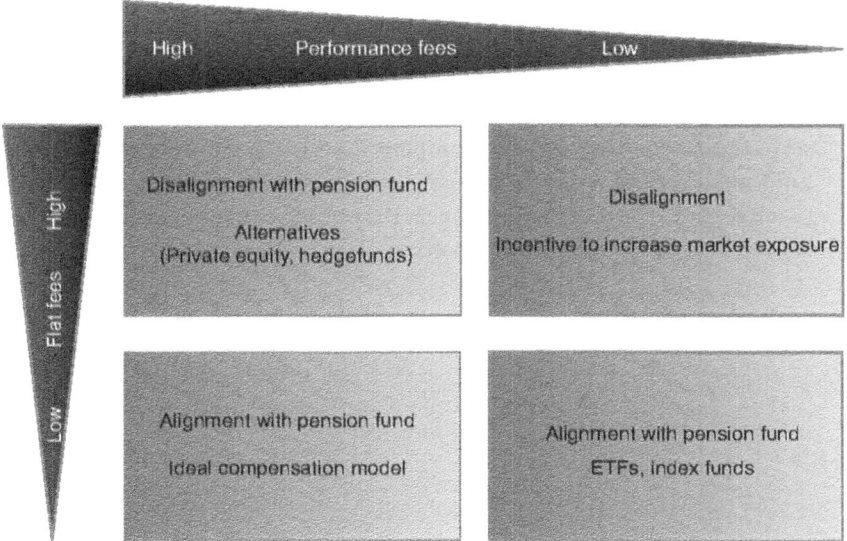

Figure 12.2   How fees affect the alignment between pension fund and asset manager

12.3　Debates to be aware of

- Financial products are like Prada and Gucci bags: entrepreneurs (or forgers if you will) jump at the opportunity to copy the new bags and sell them for a much lower price. Indistinguishable to experts and only the lucky owner knows the real value. Wait long enough, and new low-cost alternatives for any new strategy will develop by themselves. An example is hedge funds. If we look at the returns of hedge funds the question arises as to whether they are really due to skill and therefore not replicable as hedge funds managers claim, or rather just a clever combination of market exposures to equities, bonds, etc. and therefore replicable? Recent research suggests that their returns are just due to a clever combination and can be replicated with lower-cost index funds. For example, Barclays Capital has investigated whether it can provide alpha strategies at low cost, and estimates that it should be able to replicate between 50 and 100 strategies that hedge funds follow.[21] An alternative is Exchange Traded Funds (ETF), offering exposure to a wide range of index exposures of different assets with low costs. ETFs can also offer pension funds exposure to alternative investments. Funds can spend a lot of money on buying into commodities, hedge funds and property. ETFs can provide less risky and more liquid ways of investing in these areas at lower fees.[22]
- There are visible costs and hidden costs. The latter category is euphemistically dubbed "soft dollars." Assume, for example, there is a fund manager who is keen to conduct research for Citigroup. He could then agree with Citigroup to conduct his trades with it not at the lowest commission, but at one that sort of "compensates" Citigroup for awarding the fund manager the research. Industry groups have spoken out against this practice, but it still exists. Managers that hold strong beliefs about costs should also be explicit on soft dollars.

13
Organization

Summary

✓ A well-thought-out vision and design of your organization makes the difference between merely good execution and adding value.

✓ Key organizational decisions are about in/outsourcing, the role of teams and the role of innovation.

✓ The main challenge is to strike a balance between the resources and skills that the organization needs internally and the resources and skills that it wants to attract from outside the organization.

13.1 Case study

Innovation in investments comes in many guises as an investment belief. Strikingly, for the Dutch civil servants pension fund ABP, this is the faces of pop stars. In its constant search for new investment strategies, ABP bought several music catalogs in 2008 from Universal Music Group, the world's largest music company. This way ABP became the first pension fund to invest in music rights. Approximately 90,000 songs also include hits of Bon Jovi, Beyonce, Madonna, and Michael Jackson.[1] The management is also non-traditional: CP Masters, a large Dutch music publisher, became responsible for actively managing the catalogs.[2] ABP expects a return of about 8% annually.[3]

The acquisition makes perfect sense to Ronald Wuijster, head of Strategy and Research of APG investments, the pension fund's investment management company: "We believe there is an early mover advantage in searching for new asset classes."[4] Music rights provide stable and real cash flows and the long-term return potential fits the investment horizon of ABP. This was aptly illustrated when the death of pop idol Michael Jackson in 2009 belatedly boosted the popularity of his songs and accordingly ABP's revenues from the music rights.[5] Another aspect is that music rights as an asset class enhance diversification as they are by nature uncorrelated to the more traditional asset classes. However, there are quite some entry barriers to setting foot in the market for music rights: the market lacks liquidity and transparency. In addition, possible entrants need to have a lot of financial clout in combination with the availability of managers who possess the skills to manage a music catalog.[6]

Table 13.1 ABP's innovative strategies

Intellectual property rights	Infrastructure investments	ESG investments
Copyrights (venture stage and stable cash flow stage) • Music, film • Photos and arts • Games **Patents** (venture stage and stable cash flow stage) • Chemical • Medical • Industrial • Consumer related	**Land investments** • Timberlands • Farmlands • Vineyards, recreation parks	**Carbon funds** • Clean technology **Private equity** • Renewable energy infrastructure • Micro-credits

Source: Wuijster (2008)

The initiative of investing in music catalogs stems from the ambition of ABP to take the lead in innovations in pension investing. Creating an organizational culture that has an open mindset to new ideas is crucial for innovations to become successful, but so is the subsequent implementation and embedding in the organization. In 2006, ABP paved the way by creating an innovation committee, responsible for devising and assessing ideas that would not usually be considered within ABP's investment structure.[7] Also employees of ABP investments are encouraged to bring up ideas about new investment opportunities for the innovation committee.

Currently, 2% of the total invested capital is made available for the ABP innovation committee.[8] Initiatives have included timberland, infrastructure, clean technology, private equity, patents, the already mentioned music catalogs and other intellectual property rights.[9]

For ABP, the world's third largest pension fund holding about €173 billion,[10] the allocated 2% still works out at an amount of €3.5 billion. By early 2008, only a small percentage of the available capital had yet been invested in innovation proposals.[11] With such a modest impact on total return, what does ABP gain from it?

Ultimately, ABP's innovative approach is targeting the long run when the allocation to those innovative investments is intended to be much higher. Most likely, the major benefits now lie in getting acquainted with the skills and resources that are necessary to source, securitize and manage assets in undiscovered, illiquid markets. These resources will give ABP a competitive edge in those markets before a larger investment crowd discovers them. Looking at the risk side, new asset classes will most likely benefit diversification in ABP's portfolio; certainly once the risk regarding these asset classes is properly mapped. In addition, ABP exploits its enormous size as a competitive advantage. Where most pension funds simply lack the investing power to spend such amounts on innovation, ABP is in a position to do so and has created an organization that utilizes its potential to innovate.

13.2 Theory

How much thought (and research) has gone into the organizational set-up and structure of the pension plan, and how does it manage its own or external managers? This is addressed by the organizational belief, for example the belief in the role an investment manager should play in the organization to add value, or a choice between in or outsourcing. Our research pinpoints three basic elements that investment managers have to consider:

- In or outsourcing
- The role of investment managers versus the role of the investment process
- Innovation

Table 13.2 Illustration of organization investment beliefs

HSBC asset management believes "that the best results are delivered by small teams of portfolio managers who are focused, empowered and accountable."[12]

Similarly, T. Rowe Price argues that "consistently, strong, risk-adjusted performance is, in a significant measure, the result of a stable management team."[13]

According to PensionDanmark, "the best investment results are most likely to be achieved with a relatively small and focused investment team combined with a high degree of outsourcing to external managers."[14]

13.3   In- or outsourcing?

Smaller pension funds outsource a substantial part of their activities out of necessity: costs, scale and scope advantages. For larger pension funds, outsourcing versus insourcing represents a strategic choice. Still, only a small percentage (3.2%) of pension funds' investment beliefs deal with out- versus insourcing. Asset managers have none, which also makes sense since they are the beneficiaries of pension funds' outsourcing activities. Outsourcing asset management should improve investment returns since outside investment managers are likely to bring superior professional experience and skills to the pension plan investment decisions. Moreover, contracting-out allows a retirement system to change its investment managers more easily in response to poor performance. A pension fund is likely to find it more difficult to oust inside managers for weak results than to dismiss an outside firm for comparable shortcomings. Finally, outside managers are likely to be better shielded against political pressures to pick state and local companies for investment. A comparison of internally-managed pension funds with mutual funds during the late 1970s and early 1980s revealed lower risk-adjusted returns among the former, suggesting that external management has yielded superior results in the past (Berkowitz et al. 1988).

The Dutch are currently pioneering the ultimate form of outsourcing: what they like to call *fiduciary management*. The asset manager takes over implementation, even at strategic level, leaving only policy-making for

Table 13.3   Illustration of in- and outsourcing investment beliefs

Swedish AP1 Fonden manages its assets "both internally and externally. A decisive factor in the choice between internal and external management is the ability to create a higher return (after management costs) compared to the established strategic benchmark. Management areas where the fund does not possess or has difficulty in obtaining the right expertise are managed externally."[15]

The Victorian Fund Management Corporation outsources fund management, "we utilize the skills of our in-house investment team to build investment portfolios as efficiently as possible ... Investment portfolios are constructed via a combination of in-house investment management and external fund managers. Internal management is practiced where we have the capabilities to generate superior performance net of fees."[16]

The Investment Committee of Universities Superannuation Scheme (USS) believes that external managers should be employed to complement in-house expertise and/or where in-house management is not cost effective.[17]

trustees. While this seems a good outsourcing bargain, it is not taking off as spectacularly as asset managers had hoped. Trustees fear that they will be unable to maintain control over the pension fund. Also, fees tend to increase. In Chapter 4 – why pension investors and asset managers differ – we argued that the cautious approach of trustees is fully justified, since asset managers and pension funds differ on a number of crucial issues.

British-based Create Research, an investment management research group, conducted a survey among CEOs of pension funds and asked which top five factors would have the most influence in their decision when awarding mandates to asset managers (Rajan et al. 2006). Figure 13.1 shows the results ranked in increasing order of percentages of CEOs preferring a certain factor for selecting managers. Apart from anything else, principal–agent problems can arise, and the formulation of investment beliefs matters more than ever in the governance process. For one thing, the question is whether the external manager can implement investment beliefs that trustees hold but cannot execute internally. Another question could be whether the manager holds investment beliefs that are in stark contrast with the ones held by the fund.

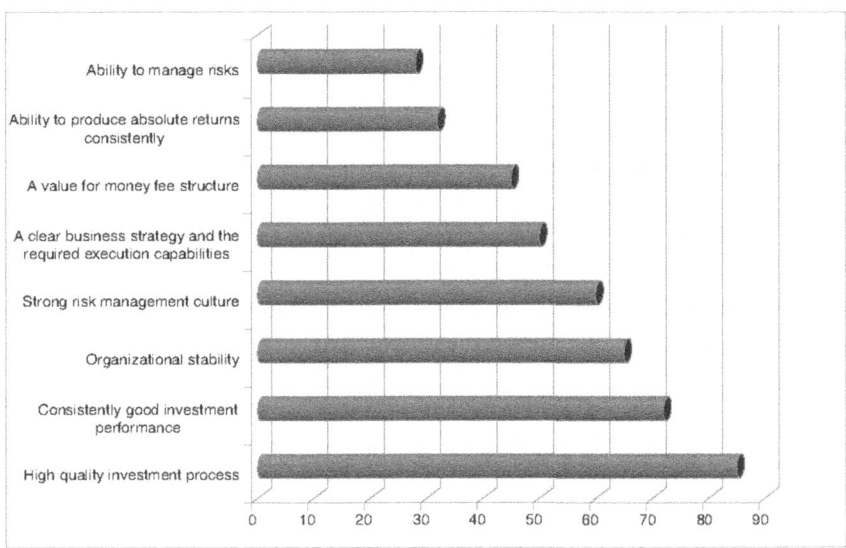

Figure 13.1 Factors influencing decisions on awarding mandates (Rajan et al. 2006). The managers surveyed were able to choose from multiple factors, hence the numbers add up to over 100%.

Meanwhile, there is growing skepticism about outsourcing. Henk Schuijt, director of Dutch Ahold pension fund, notes that a large portion of the assets under management is traditionally awarded to external investment managers, earning them handsome fees and salaries in London and New York. Disappointingly, only in 20% of the cases is the promised outperformance for the pension fund actually delivered. Schuijt therefore argues that smaller pension funds, managing 1–2 billion euro assets, should stick to at least partial internal management – saving their funds between €5–10 million in fees if 50% is managed internally.

13.4   Teams, role of investment managers

Pension funds – with the exception of the largest ones in the world – either have fully outsourced their investment management, or employ a relatively small investment staff to manage and or monitor the pension investments. A major advantage of having your own investment staff is that it provides the fund with countervailing power for the oversight of external mandates, since financial markets are monitored just as closely in-house as the external manager is expected to.

The role of investment managers and their teams is for some large pension funds and asset managers at the core of their strategy. Today's financial markets change extremely rapidly; a lengthy process of formulation and adaptation of investment beliefs is not going to work. By the time a new strategy is generated and the organization restructured, the environment will have changed many times. Ex ante investment beliefs and strategy formulation from the top is pointless; the necessary information about markets and technologies is not directly available to trustees and management operating at a high level, and it cannot be comprehended with sufficient speed and clarity to be utilized (e.g. Roberts 2004). Organizations are therefore built around investment teams.

There is always a debate about the pros and cons of an integrated top-down investment process and matching organizational structure versus a bottom-up asset-based organization structure. Australian institutional investment manager QIC, managing over $48 billion, believes that diversified and independent thinking across asset classes is central to QIC's approach to investment. "Thus we operate as a 'Village of Boutiques' with each asset class operating with a high level of autonomy. Each asset class team undertakes its own research and arrives at its own views on markets. We believe this delivers superior and more consistent performance."[18]

13.5   Innovation

Innovation is a key characteristic that many organizations firmly put high up on their banner, and it has several dimensions. First, how important is innovation to your organization? Is it innovation for finding a better mousetrap, innovation to fine-tune/redesign the investment process, or does the organization innovate to access new markets and strategies to gain first-mover advantages? The answer to this strategic question determines whether innovation is a supporting activity in the investment process, or at the heart of it.

Second, while innovation seems to be a "good" thing in general, the post-bubble policy agenda is bound to address important questions to banks and institutional investors. Is financial innovation a blessing or a curse? The merits of financial innovation are undoubtedly substantial. It has been a central force driving the global financial system towards greater efficiency. The opportunities for risk sharing have increased immensely, while transaction costs and information and agency costs have come down, resulting in considerable economic benefits. On the other hand, many economists have recently pointed to these changes in the financial markets as the root cause for the financial crisis that originated in 2008, with a magnitude and scope not seen in nearly 80 years (Merton 2009). In this respect, financial innovation can be viewed as a learning process, in which mistakes inevitably will be made now and then (Boston University 2009). Given that it is at the very least a double-edged sword, should innovation in finance be curbed, or kept far removed from the conventional investment management industry? Buyers of mortgage backed securities and subprime mortgages believed they bought into innovation based on the promise of home ownership. Holders of these innovations today face reputational risks through their realized losses and the critical questions of stakeholders.

On the other hand, innovation satisfies a genuine demand from large institutional investors. They have the resources and the slack to take on new investments, and by doing so are able to position themselves as attractive employers.[19] Innovation challenges the capabilities of the organization. At the extreme are relatively new assets, for which almost no past data is available. The data has no statistical significance and is not a meaningful basis for making rational decisions. But an investor who waits for better data to become available is actually waiting for that asset sector to become more efficient after more information leads to better pricing of the value and risks of the investment,

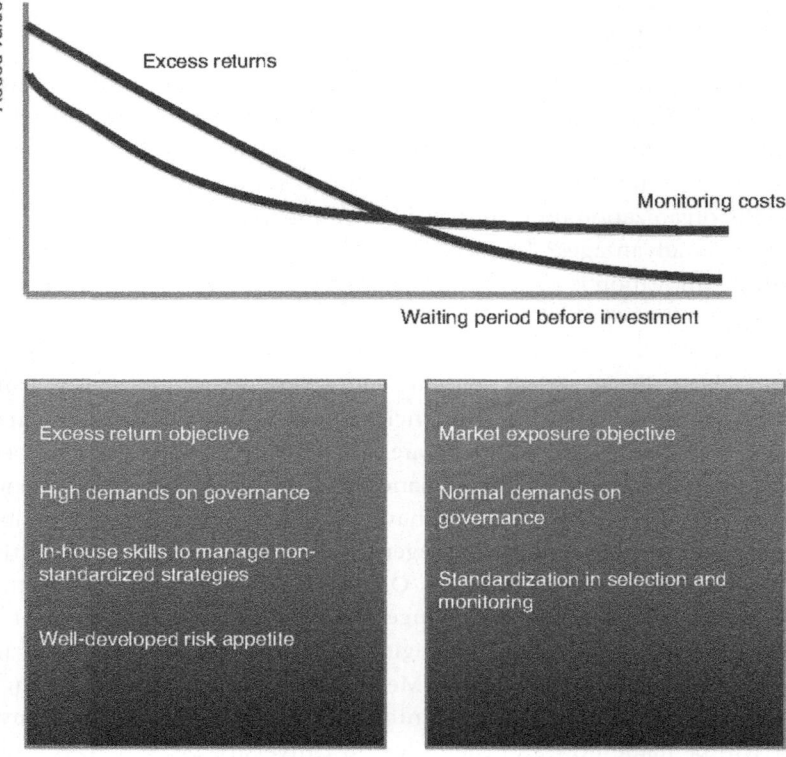

Figure 13.2   Trade-off within innovation

by which time arbitrage has extracted most of the potentially enhanced returns.

Innovation in a practical sense here means sourcing these new strategies, setting up a team and resources to facilitate this, and developing an organizational process whereby the investor can establish the trade-offs between the costs of waiting too long (lower enhanced returns but also lower monitoring cost and more comfort feeling in risk management) versus the immediate costs of entering too early, raising potentially enhanced returns but at the same time raising due diligence and monitoring costs (see Figure 13.2). This trade-off strongly depends on the governance and the resources of the investor. An innovation is like an investment with high returns but a lot of risk.

Building own resources is one approach, but another complementary one is to build strategic partnerships to develop new ideas. The ones with

the highest impact and commitment are joint ventures and financial sub-
sidiaries. Funds and endowments usually have a small capital base and
tend to build alliances. The network organization is firmly embedded
within management theory. However, funds still need to have a clear focus
on what to get out of it, and how it bolsters their own added value.

14
Sustainability

Summary

✓ Sustainability is becoming a fact of life. Institutional investors are increasingly engaged in socially responsible investments (SRI). However, as yet only a few firms hold explicit beliefs on sustainable investments.

✓ Investing in SRI funds and strategies does not necessarily differ from traditional strategies in terms of risk and return. Rather, it is a matter of aligning funds' values and investment beliefs.

✓ Pension funds can use SRI as a – moral – end in itself, but can also use it as an investment style, adding long-term value to the fund.

14.1 Saving the world and earning along the way

Al Gore's words on his departure from politics reveal a clear message: "I am very happy with what I'm doing. I enjoyed my time in public service but that's over, and I'm really enjoying the business world and having a lot of fun."[1] The former US Vice President does not seem to miss his political career at all. Besides his heavy schedule of speeches about climate change, Gore has some other activities. For example, he holds positions on the boards of directors of high-profile and successful companies Apple and Google, but even more interestingly, he has set his cap at the investment world, and business is thriving.

In 2004, Gore founded the asset management company Generation Investment Management ("Generation") together with David Blood, who was at that time CEO of the Asset Management department at Goldman Sachs.

When Gore met Blood it appeared that they had similar valuable insights about investing, though each from a different angle. Blood: "When I met Al, I discovered that we had similar goals. He was coming at it from an environmental and sustainability angle; I was coming at it from the mainstream finance side, with a strong personal interest in sustainability issues."[2] It is obvious that Gore's widespread visions on social and environmental issues play an eminent role in Generation's investment practices. The combination of their beliefs led to Generation's mission to show how integrating sustainability research into a long-term investment strategy could strengthen fundamental investment analysis.[3]

Sustainability in itself is nothing new; there are plenty of investment firms which are specialized in sustainability research, but Blood and Gore argue that it is wrong to separate it from mainstream traditional financial analyses as many firms do.[4] "The notion that business is separate from the issues such as climate change or poverty is just fundamentally flawed,"[5] they say. This makes Generation's approach unique in the investment business.

Furthermore, sustainability is not just environmental or ethical screenings of companies, but is about looking outside the narrow confines of quarterly reports[6] at further information that additionally has great significance for future company performance. Such factors include issues regarding environment, climate change, corporate culture, community engagement, but also issues like brand management, alignment of interest between company management and its stakeholder and how companies attract and retain employees.[7] The idea that these factors need to be fully integrated within the framework of traditional investment analysis is just common sense. Gore: "Proper valuation of automobile stocks is also not possible without considering long-term issues such as carbon intensity, right?"[8]

Unlike some traditional socially responsible investing approaches however, Generation is not willing to sacrifice returns to save the world.[9] Instead, Blood and Gore will proudly admit that it is Generation's main purpose to deliver superior investment performances;[10] and they say sustainable factors are right at the heart of long-term business performance.[11]

This long-term business performance plays an eminent role in Generation's investment practices as Generation's sustainable criteria to evaluate firms are designed to discover those firms that have an enduring capacity to create value and sustain competitive advantages.[12] Firms focusing too much on the short term increasingly face the risk of trailing their competitors after a while. Gore: "Ford and General Motors for example, lacked sustainable criteria and they have missed the long-term shift in consumer preferences and societal preferences towards more efficient automobiles with much less pollution."[13]

So, Generation explicitly moved away from the focus on short-term performance[14] displayed by numerous other fund managers. Quite often a long-term approach is however completely in line with the interests of clients such as pension funds for whom it is in many cases viable to take on a long-term view. Gore argues that this alignment of interests is a prerequisite for strong long-term performance and therefore it is also an essential part of sustainable investing. The alignment of Generation's interest with those of its clients has also been made explicit via its cost structure; Generation charges clients a base fee, which covers its costs, and a performance fee measured against the MSCI World Index on a three-year rolling base.[15] Moreover, Generation's founding partners initially experimented with managing their own money before attracting outside capital in 2004.

Although there are some skeptics regarding the approach of Generation and no long-term data is available to judge its performance over longer periods,[16] Blood and Gore are convinced that recognizing and applying sustainable factors will be essential for business performance over the next decades. The signs already point in their direction: within just four years Generation's Global Equity Fund attracted more than $5 billion and it had to be closed to new investors as additional inflows of capital would exceed Generation's capacity.[17] Also Generation's other fund, the Climate Solution Fund, is doing well. Generation's concept is particularly successful outside the US Blood: "Generation had very significant success with its message in Europe and Australia" and "in terms of bringing new clients in, we're ahead of what we hoped to do."[18] By early 2008, 80% of Generation's less than 100 clients were institutional clients, equally spread over Europe, Australia and the US.[19]

With respect to precise performance numbers Blood and Gore keep it strictly quiet: "That's something between us and our clients."[20] However, Gore was willing to hint that Generation's funds have returned very well for their clients since its foundation.[21] Also Mistra, a Swedish Foundation for Environmental Research and client of Generation, acknowledged that over 2008 Generation did comparatively well and that this was not the first year that Generation distinguished itself.[22]

Anyhow, there is no lack of ambition at Generation, as it wants to prove that its investment philosophy allows us to generate excess returns over the MSCI World Index of between 9% and 12% over a three-year period.[23] Gore: "We went this way because we feel it is a better way to manage money. It's not a feel good exercise. Sustainability research integrated into a rigorous traditional investment process will deliver superior long-term results."[24]

14.2   Theory

Socially responsible investment has gained headway in recent years, and is a true investment belief about the role and influence of today's pension funds in capital markets. Some even see a role for SRI in resolving future financial crises. James Gifford, executive director of the United Nations Principles of Responsible Investments, frames the surge in SRI in a broader framework: "This [...] is part of the solution to addressing the systemic failure that just happened", referring in the *Financial Times* to the credit crunch.[25]

Pension funds increasingly use their influence to engage with, and in some cases aggressively challenge, the management of corporations they invest in (Clark and Hebb 2004). Corporate engagement of this kind reflects a relatively new role that pension funds have chosen to take on. In the 1970s and 1980s SRI was limited to single issues like the South African divestment campaign; today, pension funds are increasingly engaged in a wide range of initiatives to raise firm-level standards and attract attention to a range of environmental and social issues (Table 14.1).

Pension funds' attitudes towards SRI began to change in the mid-1990s, when sweatshop labor exploitation by US companies like Nike made headlines. At the same time, public opinion portrayed oil companies negatively, for example criticism attracted by Royal Dutch Shell following the execution of Nigerian activist Ken Sarowiwa, who had been protesting against environmental damage caused by the oil industry.[26] The plans to sink the Brent Spar oil platform sparked another outcry from institutional investors. Human rights and environmental issues are major cornerstones for SRI. Today, SRI encompasses a wide range of funds, strategies and consultancies, pursuing common goals, differing widely in implementation and underlying vision.

That's because perceptions about SRI vary across countries and cultures; SRI is also defined and practiced in different ways. The systematic investigation of factors influencing SRI, and how to apply this to a portfolio or investment strategy, is still at an embryonic stage (Louche and Lydenberg 2006). For trustees, the debate about incorporating SRI in the fund is still not resolved satisfactorily. For example, should SRI be considered part of the fiduciary duty? Does SRI improve, or least not worsen, the risk-return profile of the portfolio? And, equally important, what is an effective strategy for implementing SRI?

The debate about whether SRI is part of fiduciary duty has abated to some extent, with pension industry bodies like the English Association of Pension Funds (NAPF) indeed opting to view it as part of fiduciary duty.

Table 14.1   Socially Responsible Investment (SRI) initiatives

Initiative	Founded in	Purpose	Participants
PRI	2005	United Nations backed group of institutional investors that develop and monitor the principles for responsible investments of which firms can become a signatory.	563 signatories
Pharma Initiative	2003	Dialogue between pharmaceutical companies and institutional investors to create a fairer distribution model for medicines in emerging markets.[27]	Pension funds and healthcare companies
Marathon Club	2006	Encourages pension funds, endowments and other institutional investors to be more long-term in their thinking and actions, and place more emphasis on social responsibility.	18 members
Enhanced Analytics	2004	Promotes the growth of extra-financial, quality, long-term research as well as ensuring this is integrated into the research process of fund managers.	27 members
Ceres	1989	US-based coalition of investors and environmental groups which promotes responsible corporate environmental conduct.	>50 firms

Trustees concerned with the moral dimension of socially responsible investing might seek control of corporations in order to deliver a set of outcomes from the firm that have a broad impact on the society (Clark and Hebb 2004). In theory, trustees might even decide to give up risk or return objectives to achieve a non-financial goal (Ghilarducci 1994). Restrictions and constraints on the investment universe in order to incorporate sustainable goals will create sub-optimal risk-return combinations compared to the best portfolios that are managed without any considerations other than risk-adjusted return.

Most pension funds however sidestep the role of SRI in relation to fiduciary duty and stress the financial aspects. The return-risk merits of this investment belief are hotly debated, as is the question of the most efficient application to portfolio management. In theory, investment decisions are made on the basis of the expected risk-adjusted rates of return with the stream of future cash flows embedded in current prices. However, the longer the time horizon over which pension funds hold their investments, the more (research) effort the funds have to make to minimize future risks. They believe in companies that behave in accordance with certain social, ethical or environmental standards in order to minimize these future risks and maintain, or even increase, value over the long term.

For funds shaping SRI as one of their investment beliefs, three (non-exclusive) views emerge (De Graaf and Slager 2009):

- *Ethics* and investment strategies should be fully aligned. When a fund applies its own ethical standards to investment decisions, ethical standards outweigh the effects of risk and return.
- *Financially-driven* strategies for Environment, Social and Governance (ESG) focus foremost on the return/risk trade-off. Relevant ESG issues are not priced in by the market at this moment, but these issues will have a relevant financial impact in the future.
- *Institutional responsibility-driven.* Institutional investors take responsibility for the functioning of financial markets; the integrity of the market is a joint responsibility of government, regulators and market participants. The expected benefits of these strategies affect financial markets as a whole and only by implication the funds that are invested in them.

14.2.1   Ethically-driven beliefs

When a fund applies its own ethical standards to investment decisions, ethical standards outweigh the effects of risk and return. This is only possible when trustees, the fund's participants and stakeholders develop and maintain a strong values and beliefs structure within the organization as a success factor behind implementing SRI strategies. Ethically-based strategies, however, invoke criticism as they allow stakeholders to promote their own goals by deploying the capital of beneficiaries and bypass the question about the financial rationale behind the investing. The traditional ethically-based strategy typically excludes securities from the universe to invest in; current ethically-based policies increasingly combine exclusion and a policy based on SRI-ratings, helping to define the universe to invest in. For example, the Norwegian Petroleum Fund restricts investments in the weapons industry and countries that violate human rights.

14.2.2   Financially-driven beliefs

Pension funds do not use SRI as an (moral) end in itself, but transform it into an investment style, with a set of attributes that add long-term value to the firm they invest in, and by extension to its shareholders (Clark and Hebb 2004). Environment, society and governance are integrated as among the factors in mainstream, alpha-driven strategies. Derwall et al. (2005) investigate 103 German, British and American ethical mutual funds for the 1990–2001 period. After adjusting for investment style, they find that risk-adjusted returns of ethical and conventional funds are similar. So investing in SRI is something of a call option – it produces normal returns, but has the potential to add more value to the investment in the long term. That said, ethical funds do represent a different investment style. Ethical funds contain more growth-oriented and less value-oriented companies compared with conventional funds. The reason for this may lie in the exclusion of traditional value sectors like chemicals, energy and basic industries. These sectors represent high environmental risks, and SRI fund managers tend to underweigh this. In other words, SRI alters the investment style, but not the performance.

14.2.3 Institutional responsibility-driven beliefs

However, SRI can be considered a true investment belief when the organization links sustainable investments with a long-term view of the capital markets and society. Supporters of sustainable investments either believe that there is a "capital gap" to be filled or that a "sacrifice" is required (Ghilarducci 1994). Capital gaps are caused by market failures such as information asymmetries: investors do not take into account all relevant information or do not price the information correctly, creating incorrect combinations of risk and return for different stocks or sectors; proponents of the efficient market on the other hand argue that at any time, the market price reflects the fundamental value of the firm. Sustainable investors believe that companies with adequate sustainable policies on average deliver superior earnings, and that they will

Table 14.2   Illustration of sustainability in investment process investment beliefs

OMERS believes that "well-managed companies are those that demonstrate respect for their employees, the environment, the communities in which they do business and for human rights, as well as meeting financial standards."[28]

The New Zealand Superannuation Fund believes that "long-term financial performance can be affected by environmental, social and governance (ESG) issues. We will encourage the companies we invest in to meet international standards in these areas."[29]

"PGGM has a Responsible Investment Policy aimed at integrating environmental, social and governance (ESG) factors in all investment decisions and activities."

be rewarded with above-average investment returns. However, sustainable investments seem to provide risk-return characteristics at least comparable to "normal" investments (Derwall et al. 2005).

Some of the most spectacular corporate collapses and losses in recent memory have highlighted the role that *sustainability and corporate governance* practices play in maintaining viable entities, and safeguarding investors' interests. Corporate governance was pioneered in the 1980s by the California Public Employees Retirement System (CalPERS), with $277 billion of assets under management at end-2008 – one of the world's largest pension funds.[30] CalPERS increasingly became frustrated because it was not able to exercise its shareholder rights because company management effectively blocked it. CalPERS began fighting "green mail" in the early 1980s, and activities evolved to include subjects like executive compensation, auditor independence, separation of board chairman from management, proxy voting, and developing a Focus List program of engagement, education and influence.[31]

The policy paid off. In the late 1990s, activism became an alpha generator. Research carried out by CalPERS on the effects of the system's Focus List suggests that efforts by investment funds to improve the governance of companies which are considered poorly governed also produces returns in excess of market performance. For corporate governance structures to work effectively, shareowners must be active and prudent in the use of their rights. In the 1990s, more institutional investors got involved in corporate governance for several reasons (Alexander et al. 2007): their assets under management increased, they shifted their asset allocation increasingly to equities, and moved into indexed investing. This required a new approach. Traditionally, shareholders had expressed their disapproval by selling their holdings ("The Wall Street Rule"). As institutional investors grew in size, their sheer size made it increasingly difficult to sell, giving them an incentive to influence company management. On the other hand, the move towards more indexing further constrained investors from radically adjusting their portfolios. Listed companies grew in size at the same time, reducing hostile takeovers as a potential disciplinary mechanism for failing company management. Recent discussions on executive CEO compensation are an apt example of this failing discipline mechanism. However, shareholders are gradually stepping into this void, pressing ahead on a wide range of issues from compensation to board election procedures.

The pioneering efforts by CalPERS to enhance corporate governance produced a strong link between good corporate governance and strong profitability and investment performance measures (cf. Smith 1996). This effect however wears off (cf. Nelson 2006), as most companies are having to

Table 14.3 Illustration of sustainability and corporate governance investment beliefs

Pension manager Hermes' approach is based on the belief that "companies with concerned and involved shareholders are more likely to achieve superior long-term returns than those without."[32]

The OMERS board believes "that well managed companies with strong governance processes generally produce better long-term investment returns. [...] investing in these types of companies is in the best interest of the Funds."[33]

adopt good governance practices. The empirical evidence shows that institutional investors have moderate success in pressing boards to accept reforms. There is little evidence that this has resulted in improving company performance or stock prices. Some argue that the efforts are counterproductive, and that it is a distraction for boards.

14.3   Debates to be aware of

It is far too early to tell whether investing in SRI is a new investment paradigm, as its proponents claim, or merely a combination of investment styles and exploiting (long term) anomalies in the financial markets. Environmental, social and governance (ESG) might even increase in importance for unrelated reasons. The move towards sustainable investments could, for example, also ward off more restrictive regulation of financial markets, allowing investors to stand up and say what they are going to do.[34] Minor (2007) suggests four reasons why optimism should be subdued:

- Selection bias. The past research on SRI funds followed 100 funds at the most out of a universe of thousands. The small subset might have focused on SRI factors in relatively less covered markets or smaller capitalization. As the number of SRI funds continues to grow, they will as a group increasingly mimic market performance.
- Pay-off structure. SRI managers might have an incentive to have a different pay-off structure. Some research shows that different incentive structures in SRI mutual funds tend to systematically enhance fund returns – such as lower base fees, or fees linked to long-term performance.
- Skills bias. SRI managers might show a systematic bias or trait that affect their performance. For example, Chevalier and Ellison (1999) show that managers with higher SAT scores, a standardized test for college

admissions in the US, also show higher risk-adjusted returns. In other words, SRI might attract a different set of investment managers.
- There is no such thing as *the* SRI strategy. SRI affects the investment process in different ways. Trustees can hold financial, ethical and value-enhancing beliefs behind SRI.

Investors often believe that the SRI research literature provides results that conflict with each other, reinforcing the argument that there is no such thing as *the* SRI strategy. However, based on a wide ranging literature study, Derwall et al. (2010) find that the existing research focuses on just on particular element or doctrine of SRI, ignoring the development that SRI now serves the needs of a heterogeneous group of investors, whose (financially and ethically-driven investment) views are complementary in the short run. In the long run however, it is questionable whether both views can co-exist. Financially driven SRI strategies, for instance focused on strong employee relations, represent an investment style. These strategies perhaps produce above average risk adjusted returns in the short term, but empirical evidence suggests average risk adjusted returns in the long term. While the financial logic might disappear, the values behind ethically driven investment strategies probably won't. Herein lies perhaps the real SRI challenge for trustees to formulate their beliefs.

Part III
Embedding Beliefs

Articulation of investment beliefs and an investment philosophy not only provides the right underpinnings for asset allocation, but is also an integral part of the governance of the investment organization. Having worked through Part II, Exploring Beliefs, we have provided you with the investment beliefs that form the basis for a reasoned argumentation for your investment philosophy. We examined investment beliefs from the world's leading fund managers, pension plans and endowment funds. These are the companies that appear on everybody's short list when buying asset management services, and are viewed as excellent companies in the asset management industry. Together they provide a broad based and coherent picture of today's state of the art views on asset management.

Part III – Embedding Beliefs – homes in on execution. We show how managers can use these investment beliefs to sharpen the competitive edge of their companies. We confront managers in the financial services industry with a thought-provoking question: are their asset management organizations really looking at the right things? Are their organizations attuned to a set of investment beliefs that can stand the test of time and argued debate? Do they also help direct the organization's resources to exploit the investment opportunities they believe in? These questions are at the same time the reasons why asset management companies should have these explicit beliefs. They promote transparency in goals and implementation, benefiting investors, boards of trustees and the manager. We also provide a checklist for pension fund managers on what to do when their organizations have no explicitly defined investment beliefs, but are keen to develop them for future success.

Part III

Embedding Beliefs

15
How to Hit the Ground Running

Summary

✓ It is easy for trustees to be intimidated by investment issues because there is a great deal of jargon.

✓ Trustees should resist this temptation and formulate what their investment beliefs are in plain language for asset managers. Mutual understanding of each other's beliefs determines the success of long-term relations.

✓ This chapter offers you a basic list of investment beliefs that helps you to spur the discussion in your fund.

✓ Just defining your beliefs adequately is not enough; you also need the governance to implement and monitor the beliefs.

Not all investment beliefs are born equal. American asset manager Vanguard believes in low cost and index replication. Canadian endowment fund Edmonton Tel considers strategic asset allocation as its main decision-making tool, whereas Swiss private bank Pictet uses a bottom-up approach for security selection. Tactical asset allocation is crucial for Danish pension insurer PensionDanmark, whereas Edmonton Tel believes that limited value is realized from tactical asset allocation shifts. Clearly, these organizations hold widely differing investment beliefs. Asset managers have to be aware of pension funds' investment beliefs and vice versa, if they are aiming for successful long-term relationships.

Trustees from pension funds have their fiduciary duties and the participants to consider, forming a different framework for viewing developments in financial markets than that of commercial asset managers, who have their commercial interests and clients to consider.

15.1   How hedge funds spur governance

In retrospect, 2008 might well turn out to be the year in which aligning governance, investment beliefs and organizations made its major break-through. We can thank the hedge fund industry for that. In a short period, they showed the damage that could be done by assuming implicit invest-ment beliefs, and not asking the right questions. Hedge fund strategies have been around since the Second World War, and started out as capital preservation strategies (hence the initially soothing term "hedge"). Their growth took off in the late 1970s, when risk management and pricing tools were developed (notably options pricing), and markets were deregulated, allowing a multitude of investment strategies. For asset managers, hedge funds are an ideal career opportunity: intellectually challenging, and finan-cially rewarding, due to the infamous 2/20 (2% fixed fees and 20% perfor-mance fees) business model. Their main clients, pension funds, were increasingly keen to add hedge funds to their portfolio. They seemed finan-cially rewarding (stable performance based on skills rather than market fluctuations), and upped the status of the funds – investing in hedge funds implied savvy trustees on top of their game. The years 2007 and 2008 spoiled the rosy picture. Hedge funds, in their eagerness to increase perfor-mance, took on market exposure rather than skills, and were subsequently hit hard in their returns in 2008. Many funds closed down their businesses, and trustees had to report disappointing losses to enraged participants.

But trustees now also had to face some challenging issues and go soul-searching. Did the board and pension fund organization really know what the hedge funds were up to? Could they explain it to their participants? Did they have the skills and governance process to manage the principal–agent problem? Were hedge funds a true source of diversification, or was it just more of the same, but repackaged? Is the benchmark not set unreal-istically low, and ex ante costs unrealistically high? Funds that did their homework were considered dull at the time but now look visionary. Investigating hedge funds in 2005, some pension funds concluded that while they might seem an attractive business case as such, they them-selves did not have the governance in place to monitor them and could not appreciate the high cost base; nor could they find the participants to support these type of investments. There you have it – investment beliefs in practice.

15.2   Governance leads investment philosophy

Developing a sound set of investment beliefs is crucial, as is having an organization to implement and monitor these investment beliefs. If risk management is a central investment belief, your organization should have a risk budgeting process in place to measure and manage all steps of the investment process. This is a so-called "no-brainer." Similarly, diversification as a belief only makes sense if you are willing to make the effort to investigate what really drives diversification, and understand how adding new strategies improves diversification. There are several "no brainers" in investment management when shaping an investment philosophy – including investment beliefs with a sound footing in practice and academic literature that provides you with a good basis.

Each scheme ought to suit its investment strategy to its governance resources. Rather than everyone aiming to include the newest alternative strategies around, some schemes should stick to buying or tracking market indices in familiar asset classes. It is crucial to select the most suitable level of sophistication, not the highest possible one. Switching from active to passive mandates not only acknowledges that over the long term the index will beat the majority of active managers. It is also the right approach for funds that cannot delve deeply enough into the selection and monitoring of active managers to select the better ones around, which is the case with many smaller funds. In this chapter, we synthesize the investment beliefs discussed into a starters' kit: If I am a new trustee, or manage a fund, I should be aware of how my fund approaches these beliefs. If my fund does not have outspoken views, what is then the basic scenario to start with? We describe seven investment beliefs; these investment beliefs should be the starting point for all strategic (asset allocation) reviews and discussions. The intention should be to review these on an annual basis, although major changes should not be expected from year to year – in that case you have simply reverted to writing down your investment plan or program for the coming year.

A health warning before reading further: these investment beliefs should provide a basis for reasoned debate, and not just fancy words for your website. You can adopt them and implement the consequences in your investment strategy and organization. If your organization adopts them after discussing them, fully understanding the application as well as the limitation, then this book has achieved its goal. You have become a confident participant in the financial markets, with investment beliefs – strategies – organization fully aligned. Even better is rejecting some of these investment beliefs, or adopting them to suit your own view of the financial markets. In the next chapter, we will give you more tools to make use of these elements – self-empowerment for the trustees! Once again, fully informed and after reasoned debate. The outcome we would strongly advise against is simply adopting what we have written. There is a strong governance argument for this.

However, be aware that defining investment beliefs is not sufficient: plans can go unrealized. While in earlier years this might have gone unnoticed, stakeholders today will notice, and will hold trustees accountable. Investment beliefs formulation translates into consistency of behavior, whether or not intended (e.g. Mintzberg et al. 1995, p. 14). There are of course some nuances, depending on the level of governance in the organization. If the investment beliefs are labeled "intended strategy" and the stream of actions are labeled "realized strategy", then Mintzberg distinguishes between *deliberate* strategies (where the realized strategy equals the intended strategy), meaning precise intentions (investment beliefs) existed, and *emergent* strategies, where patterns develop in the absence of leadership (see Figure 15.1). From a pension fund's point of view – focused on controlled execution and transparency in order to remain accountable to its participants and stakeholders – emergent strategies are undesirable, unless an organizational belief like innovation plays a major role and is managed diligently – but in that case, leadership is effectively

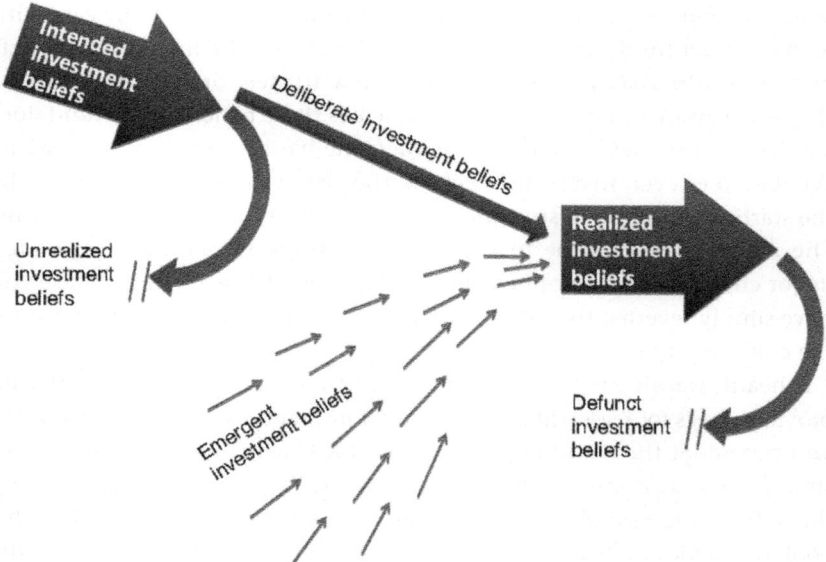

Figure 15.1   Investment beliefs formulation

being exercised. In other words, the level of governance and sophistication plays a major role.

In Chapter 3, we elaborated on investment beliefs, identifying four steps (belief – theory – strategy – organization) that help clarify discussion. When your fund does not have the resources and staff to invest to develop this, it might be practical to bundle them into two steps: (belief – theory), and (strategy – organization). Two examples demonstrate this approach:

Table 15.1   Examples of investment beliefs

	Our belief (Belief – Theory)	Consequence (Strategy – Organization)
BBC Pension Fund	There are normally additional returns available for investing in illiquid assets (the illiquidity premium). The Scheme has substantial liquidity and enjoys the benefit of positive cash flows that are expected to continue over the medium term.	The Scheme should look to exploit illiquidity more than it does at present to increase the overall returns.
Local Authorities Pension Plan	Taking risk to improve long-term investment return is both necessary and appropriate for LAPP. Setting asset mix policy is the most important investment decision – explaining about 90% of the variability of investment returns.	The Board will: • optimize investment returns over the long-term with an appropriate level of risk; • have a bias towards equities, based on an assessment of risk, to add long-term value; • examine risk/reward trade off of alternative classes and mixes of investment assets; • determine strategic long-term asset mix; and • manage it within policy ranges.

Once again, to get the debate going, this chapter offers a basic set of investment beliefs. Not to implement thoughtlessly, but to give discussions a kick-start. Table 15.2 presents seven investment beliefs that more or less summarize the debates that we've highlighted in the previous chapters.

Table 15.2   A starter's set of investment beliefs

A starter's set of investment beliefs
1. Strategic asset allocation is the most important choice in the investment process
2. Active management does not pay off
3. Costs determine net return
4. There are only a select number of risk premiums worth pursuing
5. Simplicity pays off: we match governance and strategies
6. We only invest if we agree on when to exit
7. Sustainability is an opportunity, not a necessity

Belief 1: Strategic asset allocation is the most important choice in the investment process.

It is investment theory 101, but needs to be cherished and understood anyway: the asset allocation mix decision is by far the most important determinant of the risk return allocation of the fund. This insight was developed in the 1980s, and still stands today. Trustees and investment committees should therefore concentrate on the strategic asset allocation, examine whether it is robust enough for different scenarios, and question whether a new strategy really improves diversification. These are simple questions that add more to the long-term health of a fund than anything else. (See Chapter 9 – "Impact and Focus Decisions")

Belief 2: Active management does not pay off.

The main message here is: By default, we invest in passive strategies. It is dull for the pension fund, disappointing for the asset manager, but highly rewarding for our participants. We only pursue active strategies if we know the source of anomalies, and are very confident that the (selected) manager will be able to repeatedly exploit them in the future, and is willing to agree on a performance schedule that reflects his own confidence. But even then, when external managers are involved, we need to be aware of the ex ante soberingly low probability of choosing winners. We resist the temptation to award active mandates simply because we invest in a specific region or asset. (See Chapter 5 – "Inefficiencies" and Chapter 11 – "Investment Style")

Belief 3: Costs determine net return.

The basic intuition is that, other things being equal, lower costs imply a higher net return. Costs are certain, returns are not. Many studies, investigating the core drivers for future returns, point out that costs are a critical factor in determining returns. In case a pension fund would have to choose between two similar investments, the advice would be to opt for the lower-cost alternative. However, in practice such clear choices are not available to trustees. One thing is for sure though: higher costs are never a guarantee of better performance; rather, the opposite is true. Therefore, pension fund managers should always seek to unearth all the costs attached to the investment (and focus on the hidden ones), and avoid transaction costs where possible. (See Chapter 12 – "Costs")

Belief 4: There are only a select number of risk premiums worth pursuing.

Not all risk premiums are created equal. Some risks we have to bear (inflation, interest, longevity), others we choose to bear (equity, illiquidity). We are aware that earning risk premiums is not a certainty over a longer horizon, and therefore do not blindly accept mean reversion as a fundamental. We therefore have to assess which risks we can bear, and what we should at minimum expect in return for the risk. For example, we may decide we are especially well-placed to win the equity risk and liquidity risk premium, but we believe that we are less well-placed to win the foreign exchange risk premium. (See Chapter 6 – "Risk Premiums", and Chapter 8 – "Investment Horizon")

Belief 5: Simplicity pays off: we match governance and strategies.

Pension funds invest other people's money. We are a financial institution, and our existence is based on the long-term trust of participants. No matter how complex, innovative or attractive a particular investment is, we have to be 100% accountable. If we know beforehand that we cannot live up to this ambition, we should not invest in it, however enticing the investment proposal. Our governance, investment process and risk management fully encapsulate the characteristics of the investment decisions we make, and the products and strategies that we choose. (See Chapter 10)

Belief 6: We only invest if we agree on when to exit.

We are aware of behavioral biases in financial markets, and within ourselves. We resist tendencies to repeat our mistakes in the future by specifying beforehand what we expect from an investment, how it reinforces our investment beliefs, how and when we will evaluate the results, and especially under what conditions we will exit. This is an integral part of our governance process; we do this to learn from our mistakes, improve our processes and avoid (human) mistakes. (See Chapter 11 – "Investment Styles", and Chapter 5 – "Inefficiencies")

Belief 7: Sustainability is an opportunity, not a necessity.

We believe that substantial attention should be devoted to the incorporation of social, ethical and/or environmental standards in our investments, if participants attach importance to this role. By doing so, common sense risk management drives us. We are able to minimize future risks (of holding investments for a long time period) and, consequently, increase long-term value for the fund and, by extension to its participants and stakeholders. We will use both negative screening and positive screening to select the most sustainable investment strategies. For example, well-governed markets and companies drive good returns.

16
(Re)engineering Your Own Beliefs

Summary

✓ Trustees should communicate regularly with their participants about investments. Using investment beliefs is an apt way – it helps you reiterate the message, and underpin crucial decisions.

✓ The success of a well-thought-out investment policy depends on the right roles for trustees and the fund's investment committee, and asking the right questions.

✓ This chapter helps you with checking beliefs for effectiveness, validity and coherency.

Having the right investment beliefs is crucial; so is putting them into practice. This chapter provides guidelines for trustees and investment managers for delivering the right results. The essential point throughout the book is that finance is a relatively young discipline in which data are limited, biased, or both; and in which the ratio of noise to signal is very high. It is very difficult to know anything with a degree of certainty when it comes to investment theory. Therefore we must believe certain things, be able to differentiate between what we actually know and believe, and shape strategies according to these beliefs (Denison 2008).

Articulation of investment beliefs and an investment philosophy not only provides the right underpinnings for asset allocation, but is also an integral part of the governance of the investment organization. The pension fund has to balance different interests. Pensioners and regulators increasingly demand more clarity as the invested assets accumulate further.

The investment organization on the other hand has to determine its added value, realizing that it is a pension investor, not an asset manager.

This way of managing uncertainty is relatively new, and should regularly take trustees and investors out of their comfort zone. We would rather search in the investment field for strong opinions, ignoring uncertainties that are really there, and succumbing to analyst predictions or buy and sell recommendations (cf. Sherden 1998; Morris et al. 2007).[1] Accepting and managing uncertainty should also be reflected in a coherent investment philosophy with well thought-out investment beliefs – it has to be challenged and reassessed whenever possible. We are not keen on the change for change's sake approach that many managers hold. We do however observe that there is no such thing as the financial market, but many sub-markets that have their own rises and falls. Just consider the following facts:

- In the 1950s, investing in growth stocks was the preferred strategy (the nifty fifties).
- Despite an alarming body of negative research literature, most funds invest in active mandates.
- Many pension funds have widely differing liability structures but have broadly similar asset mixes.
- Funds have added alternative investments with considerable enthusiasm. Arguments in favor are thinly spread (managers point to Yale as the hallmark of alternative investing), and the 2007–2009 crisis will surely boost the reassessment discussion.

Investment committees usually bear the brunt of these uncertainties while ensuring that the investment portfolio is properly managed. In most countries, such committees combine a number of trustees with several outside advisors, who are chosen to augment the skills of the trustees regarding investments. The committee has the (legal) responsibility for managing the fund's investments. We outline in this chapter how the formulation of investment beliefs fits into the process.

Let us make one thing clear; we are not arguing that the pension fund should draft a mission statement. Ultimate mission statements are the American Declaration of Independence. This is not what you should aim for. Ever since Peters and Waterman advised managers in the 1982 publication of *In Search of Excellence* to articulate clearer goals, the fad has gone too far.[2] We are also not propagating gems that might become contestants for the next Pulitzer prize. Rather, our goal is formulation of beliefs that help trustees form a clearer picture on where and where not to act in the financial markets.

16.1   Engineering investment beliefs

David Denison, CEO of Canadian Pension Plan, argues that the key to success for any organization is how well its strategy, governance and business practices align to its own unique beliefs, challenges and characteristics (Denison 2008). He focuses on what we can learn from ourselves. And that is a lot. The relatively low degree of published investment beliefs in our research (a mere 20% of the investigated organizations) suggests that many investment managers have yet to explicitly formulate their investment beliefs. A practical approach would be to examine the realized strategies embodied in the existing situation. Using the investment policy and other strategic documents, the organization can unearth these implicit investment beliefs and use them as a framework for evaluating the desired configuration of mission, investment beliefs, investment policy and organization. With these results in mind, has the current asset management organization the resources and competences to effectively realize an investment policy to implement these investment beliefs? Where are the gaps and which competences should be bolstered?

Any active asset manager or pension fund has a set of investment beliefs, even if not in writing. They should be made explicit, and checked to determine which investment beliefs truly apply to the asset management organization. Writing down investment beliefs requires you to take a view on capital markets.

A typical pension plan might have two goals: to execute the strategic asset allocation to achieve at least the benchmark return, and to realize outperformance on top of the benchmark return. We assume that the managed assets are broadly diversified, and a portion is managed internally. We now have to work our way backwards to retrieve the hidden investment beliefs. For example, executing the strategic asset allocation assumes that markets are highly efficient. Inefficiencies cannot be exploited in the long term. Emphasis on risk diversification, passive strategies and low costs should therefore be expected. Realizing outperformance on top of the benchmark return suggests however that the organization has a clear view of which inefficiencies or skills it can exploit: mean reversion or inefficient asset pricing strategies, or the skills to select the right external manager who can do so. Trustees should make this competence explicit.

Based on what other asset managers have produced, somewhere between four and six investment beliefs should suffice, depending on the complexity of the organization. These investments beliefs then form a sound basis for formulation of the investment policy. If you do not have a view, say so.

The soul searching process is now almost to an end. You've either developed your own beliefs, or maybe the beliefs presented in Chapter 15 – "How to Hit the Ground Running" – have triggered your organization in thinking about their own set. Once the beliefs are written down, you might check them for effectiveness, validity, and coherency:

- Do the investment beliefs form a coherent set of beliefs? Do the investment beliefs reinforce each other (e.g. efficiency of markets and cost base) or contradict each other? Do combined investment beliefs allow you to base your investment policy on them? Can the investment beliefs be identified separately in the investment process?
- Can an investment policy be designed and based on these investment beliefs? The translation of investment beliefs into investment policy should be straightforward, otherwise the investment beliefs needs to be reformulated. A practical approach is taken by Canadian Alberta Based Local Authorities Pension Plan (LAPP), running a contributory defined benefit pension plan for employees of local authorities. LAPP sets up a table where each investment belief is followed by its translation into investment policy. An investment belief of LAPP is that "taking risk to improve long-term investment return is both necessary and appropriate [...] Setting asset mix policy is the most important investment decision." To apply this investment belief, the Board will "have a bias towards equities, based on an assessment of risk, to add long-term value [...] and determine strategic long-term asset mix."
- Do the investment beliefs justify the setup of your organization? Are you able to attach tangible results to the beliefs that are reflected in the organization? If the investment management organization has named long-term mean reversion as the main inefficiency to base its strategy on, and the current strategies tend to be short term; there clearly is a misalignment. Formulating investment beliefs is the first step in identifying misalignments and correcting them.
- Finally, what may seem as an afterthought is in fact a reality check. Keeping Chapter 4 in mind: do the investment beliefs reflect the ambitions of your fund, or the asset manager's ambitions?

16.2   Communicating beliefs

Accountability to trustees, clients, and participants is steadily growing in importance. The investment beliefs should provide the investment manager with a framework to explain the choices he has made, or the choices he will have to make, enhancing the organizations' own governance. Also, it should provide clients and trustees with the proper attribution framework for judging the results.

Beliefs should be communicated – stakeholders must be clear about what strategic choices to expect from their pension fund or asset managers. Anglo-Saxon countries have a long-standing tradition of pension plans drawing up and publishing investment principles and outlining goals, objectives, and the organization of the pension arrangement. In continental Europe this is not yet commonplace; but change is underway. Also, more public pension plans than corporate pension plans tend to publish investment beliefs, reflecting a higher demand for transparency regarding these types of funds. When communicating investment beliefs, be as explicit as possible. Also, do not hesitate to communicate them to external stakeholders and professional parties your fund works with. Be sure to check beforehand:

- Do the investment beliefs represent the values expressed by your participants?
- Do they reflect your funds' skills, values, and ambitions?
- Can investment managers relate to them and communicate them?

16.3   Questions to ask

There are a number of questions to ask with respect to investment beliefs. Which questions you have to ask depends on your role and activities:

- When you are an investment committee of a pension fund.
- When selecting external mandates.
- When you are an asset manager dealing with a pension fund.
- When you're communicating with your stakeholders.

16.3.1   When you are an investment committee of a pension fund

Keep an open mind. Invite staff and outside experts to challenge your ideas. To be an effective committee, it should (Morrell 2006):

- Focus on its strategic mission; understand the role and importance of the fund to the financial well-being of the participants and sponsor.

- Function as a team.
- Set a proper agenda.
- Set an objective measure of success.
- Be properly informed.
- Develop a cooperative relationship with institutional management.

Broad investment policy is the domain of the board of trustees. An *investment policy* should document the issues that the committee must address, concentrating on the desired outcomes. The investment policy's main focus is on the asset mix relative to the liabilities. The policy addresses the following (cf. Anson 2005):

- The strategic mission of the investments.
- The core investment beliefs.
- The return objective.
- The level of risk tolerance.
- The asset classes to be included in the portfolio.
- A methodology for rebalancing the portfolio.
- Manager selection vision.
- The asset mix ranges of the portfolio's various asset classes.

The investment policy is intended as a basis for developing and adhering to appropriate investment strategies on a long-term basis. The development of a series of core investment beliefs serves as a guide for decision-making and ensures that all members of the committee share common values and assumptions. Lacking core beliefs laid out in writing usually results in disagreements that often cause uncoordinated actions. An effective committee is one that shares written core beliefs and relies on them to guide the investment process.

The investment policy not only draws the strategic outline for the investment committee to achieve the fund's long-term goals. It also helps the fund deal with the various parties who are concerned with the fund's investment return: participants, sponsor(s), regulators, and other non-committee trustees of the fund. In the European Union, drawing up and publishing an investment policy became mandatory as of 2003, although minimum standards have not been outlined.[3]

The drafting of the investment policy should be tailor-made for the fund, and is not as complex as it sounds. Just by looking at the current portfolio, you will be able to distill the implicit beliefs. Writing them down induces the next step: do you agree with these beliefs? Does your fund have the resources, skills, and risk appetite for implementing them? Equally important, are they actually your beliefs, or do they in fact just reflect what your asset manager does? Chapter 4 investigated how investment beliefs differ for pension funds and asset manager. A goal for an asset manager might just be a means to an end for the fund. For example, pension funds do not crave for "alpha" returns, just as most of us do not really crave a hammer and a nail. The hammer and nail are just unavoidable tools for putting a picture on the wall, which is what you really want. So the questions for the investment policy are what you really want (higher stable returns), what tools you need, and what tools you can do without.

It is the investment managers' role to convince you of the new investment strategy or instrument. And most of the time, that is a good thing. We manage portfolios in a far more informed way and with much better tools than we did ten years ago. But, again, the investment manager's interests are not fully aligned with those of the fund. So ask yourself, if you cut the expected rewards by half, would you still hire the new external manager? When he projects 0.6% excess return per annum, would you settle for 0.3% and still hire him? In other words, manage your own managers' expectations. Which usually means toning them down.

While the investment committee's main responsibility is setting the broad investment policy and developing investment beliefs, it should also keep a watchful eye on the *operating policy,* where investment beliefs are implemented. The operating policy serves as an operational blueprint for action, or "who does what". Roles are clearly defined. Strategic asset allocation is performed by the board of trustees of a pension fund. Tactical asset allocation is performed by the investment staff. Sub-asset classes should be left to the implementation stage. The main operational issues concern:

- Execution (effective strategy, decision-making, tactics, education, performance review, committee orientation, voting process, communication, committee selection, attribution analysis).
- Manager selection.
- Rebalancing activities.
- Asset mix.
- Monitoring risk controls, derived from the execution activities.

16.3.2   When selecting external mandates

Once investment beliefs are discussed and agreed upon, a next step for investors is to consider the extent to which the consequences are integrated

(Mercer 2007) into current investment management. Two strategic questions emerge for the pension fund when selecting, monitoring and evaluating external managers:

- What are our current investment managers: do they fit into our investment beliefs?
- What kind of managers do we want to hire in the future?

Minahan (2008) points out that engaging in a discussion with an investment manager by starting off with the question "what are your investment beliefs?" would probably elicit a lot of questions and not a very sensible discussion. Maybe it is better to start off by trying to shape the discussion in the form of statements/investment beliefs, and use these for further in-depth discussion. Relevant questions are: "What is the source of your alpha?" If the manager cannot describe the source of his alpha, you may want to politely end the interview. But to keep the conversation going: "What are the underlying patterns?", "Why are they not arbitraged away?" It is worthwhile to explore this in more detail. James Ware (2006) argues that firms that enjoy short-term success probably do so by following trends. And these are the funds that show up on your short list for selecting external managers. The real danger is ignoring these questions. So keep on asking:

- Does he have access to better information (in a legal way)? Does he build models that exploit information in a better way? What behavioral biases does he exploit? Can the manager show convincingly that the past returns in alpha can be linked to this source? Why should it persist in the future? Fuller notes that the nice thing about managers exploiting behavioral biases is that human behavior changes very slowly. However, it takes new whiz kids around the block and more computing power to replicate the proprietary model.
- If you are ready to change tactics during this discussion, Minahan (2008) provides an interesting twist by developing an approach based on what he calls the "inverted market theory." The basic idea of the Efficient Market Theory, still one of the most powerful theories around, is reflected in asset prices. Once new information is known, the information can no longer be used to generate superior returns. Minahan challenges investment managers with the logical construct: if you, as a manager, are able to generate superior return, you have to be able to act on value-relevant information or perspectives before that information

becomes reflected in the price. In other words, what do you see that others do not?

The organizational culture should also get a closer look. Do the potential managers support or discourage greater awareness of investment beliefs? The paradox here is that on the one hand implementation in a rigid, consistent way fosters trust in compliance and execution. However, it does nothing for the adaptive qualities of the organization. To succeed here, the organization needs to have a "loose" approach, allowing debate to emerge and critical questions to be asked, all signs that a strong capability for surfacing beliefs is present and working. A very visible sign of this is to check the external focus of the company. Are managers and analysts actively seeking outside challenges? Are they speaking and participating in round tables and seminars, and do they write critical articles that might even challenge their own current beliefs? That is, is the organization you would like to do business with – highly charged with adaptive capabilities, and a focus far beyond the standard marketing sales pitch? Besides selecting managers, an equally important part is evaluating managers. One of the key elements of having an investment beliefs system is developing a performance measurement system that is tuned to the investment belief and subsequent strategy that is followed. The challenge here is to develop metrics that reflect the investment belief. This is an extremely hard thing to do, but no reason not to push for it for the following reasons:

- However flawed the measure, and even if it is ultimately rejected, it is proof that the manager has done his best to think through the consequences.
- Measurement allows a structured debate between investor and trustee on the opportunities and limitations of the strategy, as well as a focus for discussion about when the belief should be reviewed or even discarded.

16.3.3   When you are an asset manager dealing with a pension fund

Beware of sales pitches based on past patterns. Do not sell your potential client slogans like "Low price-to-book always works in the long run" or "Blue chips are always a safe bet". This is nice stuff for historians, but inadequate for trustees, and downright misleading unless it is based on a solid analysis and grounded in theory.

Determine whether your investment philosophy represents the investment beliefs and values expressed by the pension fund and participants.

16.3.4   When you're communicating with your stakeholders

Accountability to trustees, clients, and participants is steadily growing in importance. The investment beliefs should provide the investment manager with a framework for explaining the choices he has made, or the choices he will have to make, enhancing the organization's own governance. Also, it should provide clients and trustees with the proper attribution framework for judging the results.

Beliefs should be communicated – stakeholders must be clear about what strategic choices to expect from their pension fund or asset managers. Anglo-Saxon countries have a long-standing tradition of pension plans drawing up and publishing investment principles and outlining goals, objectives, and the organization of the pension arrangement. In continental Europe this is not yet commonplace; but change is underway. When communicating investment beliefs, be as explicit as possible. Be sure to check beforehand:

- Do the investment beliefs represent the values expressed by your participants?
- Do they reflect your funds' skills, values, and ambitions?
- Can investment managers and relate to them and communicate them?

16.4   Fallacies to avoid

Before the portfolio is constructed, it is essential that the members of the committee have a clear understanding and agreement about the desired return of the fund and the acceptable level of risk necessary to achieve it. Everyone should also understand how the modeling process works and, perhaps more important, be aware of its shortcomings and limitations. Trustees should keep the following caveats in mind:

Understand legacy. So what really matters for your pension fund? An advisor recently quipped that a CEO typically inherits ten strategic decisions from the past, and is only able to add or influence two new ones during his reign. There is no reason why this should not also apply to an investment committee. Find out what the major decisions over the last five years were, what they aimed to achieve, and if this succeeded. If documentation is scarce, try reengineering (see 16.1).

Do not confuse personal investing experience with institutional investing. To what extent is the belief influenced by the personal beliefs of trustees and by wishful thinking? This matters, because trustees can for the most part no longer function based on their direct experience of handling investments in their personal portfolios (Morrell 2006). Instead, they must work hard to learn the unique characteristics of asset classes that are now available to institutional portfolios. It is not unusual for pension funds to hold as many as 15 different asset classes in their portfolios, compared to five as recently as 15 years ago.

Beware of overconfidence. Going through the process of formulating a clear investment philosophy creates a feeling of reward, but could easily turn into overconfidence. Overconfidence refers to the phenomenon that people or organizations sometimes tend to overrate their knowledge. Trustees choose investment managers for their passion and confidence of management style. Ware (2008b) observes that nearly half of the investment teams pension funds work with choose passion as a core value. A story might be conveyed with confidence, whether or not supported by good arguments, and generally pleases the investment committee or trustees (now we really have something to decide about). This is however a false certainty, a point brought home by Nicholas Taleb (2005). We make up stories to explain reality, thereby comforting ourselves. The stories might not be true however.[4]

There are millions of investors out there, but just one Warren Buffet. Chances are that your well-thought-out philosophy will not beat his track record. Learning to develop a curious attitude is the antidote for overconfidence.

Confirmation bias. However, there remain enough pitfalls down the road. Confirmation bias suggests that we, as humans, are all-to-eager to confirm our belief that we are right. Our tendency is to unconsciously look for information that supports our position. Clark et al. (2006) show that trustees are not immune to this behavioral bias. Committee members screen incoming information based on the way we as humans are hardwired and what we deem important. On the other hand, our personalities are wired to place different emphases on factors in our environment. Some people see danger everywhere – the glass is always half-empty; others always see the glass as half-full.

The Blame Game. Without any reservation, investment committees and funds should take 100% responsibility for their actions. This might seem self-evident; it is what fiduciary duty is all about. Professional investors however are constructed with a different DNA. They take credit for their successes, attributing them to skill, and they dismiss their failures, attributing them to bad luck, other people's mistakes, or adverse markets that hit everyone. It is a very subtle process. Researchers recently spelled it out from the *Wall Street Journal* (Morris et al. 2007). They found that articles about positive returns used active phrases like "the stock climbed upwards", "regained its path", or "turned the corner". These are examples of positive, skill-based terms. With negative returns, they found an abundance of stocks "spiraling downwards", "gravitating downwards", or "negative sentiment". The message here is clear: negative returns are passive – it is the market – while positive returns are active – it is due to our own decisions and skills. This trap has two negative consequences:

- It further contributes to the overconfidence bias. Trustees think they really made wonderful decisions.
- It is a powerful incentive for creating a "blame" culture in which people point fingers at others and work to avoid getting blamed themselves.

The blame culture has some unintended consequences. First, investment philosophy and strategic asset allocation will tend to be based on what the peer group decides to do, not on what is essential for the fund. This is a form of cognitive dissonance: committee members disagreeing with decisions, but not wanting to confront them. Second, it will block learning by the investment committee since a candid and open-minded performance attribution will not be possible.

Learning and improving. Given our tendency to rewrite history (the hindsight bias), we need a reliable way to monitor investment decisions, so we can later perform accurate post-mortems. It is common for committee members or investment managers not to remember exactly what their thoughts or reactions were at the time of the decision. Confronted with the realized returns, the team suffers from hindsight bias and makes up a story that comfortably fills in the gaps. Performance attribution should not just be a mechanical exercise. The rationale for all major decisions should be recorded ex ante in the minutes, whether this is a change in asset allocation or selection of a new manager.

Trade in the calendar for the ruler. Paul Trickett, head of pension consultant Watson Wyatt views this as "moving away from the historical practice of making investment decisions around dates in the diary and opt instead for investment processes that can be implemented according to predefined rules, as and when the opportunities arise."[5] Markets are becoming increasingly volatile; a financial crisis every three to four years will not be out of the ordinary. Long-term investing will increasingly mean making changes based on long-term principles. Successful committees adopt more dynamic long-term strategies. The best way is to do the thinking in advance about the market conditions in which you would make a change and set up a process for acting on a pre-agreed decision, all fitting within the right governance framework.

16.5   It's now up to you

What *Investment Beliefs* has emphasized is that managing your investment portfolio entails more than determining an asset mix and monitoring it regularly. Only a minority of organizations currently devotes sufficient time to formulating Investment Beliefs and actually understands investment principles. Organizations and trustees who do however formulate investment beliefs create a firm basis for weathering uncertain times and adapting successfully in the long term.

Investment beliefs accept the reality that economics and finance cannot be captured in hard, predictive models. Instead, they encompass a *view* on how other investors in the financial markets learn or fail to learn. The term "belief" accepts that there are no objective truths in the financial markets, and that investors can choose to interpret observations or mechanisms differently. The formulation of Investment Beliefs contributes to performance, as it helps trustees and investment managers to make informed decisions consistent with their objectives.

As we have tried to show you throughout the book, especially in Part II, formulating investment beliefs requires some stimulating and soul searching homework. What do we really mean by long-term investing, diversification? How are we to add value by active management? Do we really understand the dynamics behind risk premiums and investment styles? Academics provide guidance, but this only goes so far. Throughout the book, we have touched upon the main debates, and provided readers with recent insights.

Ultimately, trustees and investment managers need to make up their own mind what these fundamentals mean to them, and their investment process. Chapters 15 and 16 offered practical guidelines for transforming academic debates into practical investment beliefs. Funds today should not limit themselves to fine-tuning their investment processes to further improve execution, but should also adapt to changing environments.

Readers of Investment Beliefs should take these lessons to heart – and take heart from them – as they embark on their own investment beliefs journey. We hope we have inspired you.

Notes

Chapter 1   Introduction

1 <http://www.capitalspectator.com/>.
2 Excellent introductions are Freeman Ware, J. W., 2008b, Investment Process Review, Focus Consulting Group., Russell Freeman, A., 2006, *All You Need to Know About Being a Pension Fund Trustee*, Longtail Publishing Limited, London; or Murakidhar Russell, C., 2006, *Trustee Investment Strategy for Endowments and Foundations*, John Wiley & Sons, Ltd., Chichester.

Chapter 2   Think Twice About Your Investment Philosophy

1 Sophia Grene, "Few fund trustees 'consider core beliefs'", *Financial Times Fund Management*, December 3, 2007, p. 2.

Chapter 3   Uncovering Beliefs

1 It's also an adequate check for fraud. For Jerome Kervier and Nick Leeson, only the investment strategy box could be ticked. That leaves three unanswered, quite a lot for continued success.
2 Gill Wadsworth, "Analysis of skills could be better route to alpha", *Financial Times Fund Management*, May 26, 2008, p. 8.
3 ABP, retrieved from <www.abp.nl>. Kwartaalcijfers ABP, vierde kwartaal 2008, January 2009.
4 <http://www.abp.nl/abp/abp/images/Brochure%20Strategic%20Investment %20Plan%202007-2009%20doc.nr.26.1066.07_tcm108-46252.pdf>.
5 Retrieved from: <http://www.vanguard.com/international/hIndEN/research/we-believesEN.html>. Date accessed: July 29, 2009.
6 Retrieved from: <http://www.vanguard.com/international/hIndEN/research/we-believesEN.html>. Date accessed: July 29, 2009.

Chapter 4   Why Pension Investors and Asset Managers Differ

1 Simon Goodley, "Unilever and Merrill Lynch make peace", December 6, 2001, Tele-graph.co.uk, <http://www.telegraph.co.uk/finance/2744735/Unilever-and-Merrill-Lynch-make-peace.html>.
2 Carolyn Bandel, "Cost of fraud triples for Philips fund", IPE.com, August 4, 2008, <http://www.ipe.com/news/Cost_of_fraud_triples_for_Philips_fund_28738.php?ty pe=news&id=28738>.
3 The surveyed funds and asset managers were, clustered by country, from Australia (State Super Financial Services Australia, Victorian Fund Management Corporation),

Canada (Canada Pension Plan, Edmonton Tel Endowment Fund, Local Authorities Pension Plan, OMERS, Ontario Teachers Pension Plan, Public Employees Benefits Agency, Workers Compensation Board Alberta), Denmark (ATP, PensionDenmark), Germany (Deutsche Asset Management), The Netherlands (ABN Amro Asset Management, ABP, ING Asset Management, Interpolis Insurance, Metalektro, PGGM, Shell Pension Fund), New Zealand (NZ Superannuation Fund), Norway (Norges Bank Investment Management), Sweden (AP Fondsen), Switzerland (Pictet, UBS), the United Kingdom (Foreign & Colonial Asset Management, Hermes, HSBC Asset Management, Schroder Investment, University Superannuation Scheme, Axa Rosenberg), and the United States (Capital group, DGAM, Goldman Sachs Asset Management, MOSERS, Nebraska Investment Council, Northern Trust, T. Rowe Price, TIAA-CREF, Vanguard, Yale Endowment Fund).

Chapter 5 Inefficiencies

1 O'Loughlin, J. (2004), *The Real Warren Buffet – Managing Capital, Leading People*, Paperback edition, Nicholas Brealey Publishing.
2 Nocera, J. (2009), "Poking holes in a theory on markets", *The New York Times*, June 5, 2009. Retrieved from: <http://www.nytimes.com/2009/06/06/business/06nocera.html?_r=2&8dpc>. Date accessed: June 23, 2009.
3 Tully, S. (1998), "How the really smart money invests", *Fortune*, New York, July 6, 1998, Vol. 138, Iss. 1, pp. 148–151.
4 Appel, D. (2005), "Beyond theory", *Pensions & Investments*, Chicago, November 28, 2005, Vol. 33, Iss. 24, p. 32.
5 <http://www.lsvasset.com/about/about.html>. Date accessed: June 24, 2009.
6 LSV was founded in 1994 and named by its three academic founders: Josef Lakonishok, William G. Karnes Professor of Finance at the University of Illinois; Andrei Shleifer, Economics Professor at Harvard University; and Rober Vishny, former Eric J. Gleacher Professor of Finance at the University of Chicago.
7 As of 31 December 2008, <https://personal.vanguard.com/us/content/Home/WhyVanguard/AboutVanguardWhoWeAreContent.jsp>. Date accessed: June 25, 2009.
8 <http://www.vanguard.com/pdf/flgip.pdf?2210035510>. Date accessed: June 25, 2009.
9 <http://www.vanguard.com/pdf/flgip.pdf?2210035510>. Date accessed: June 25, 2009.
10 Kirby, J. (2003), "Passive but still picky", *Canadian Business*, Toronto, October 27–November 9, 2003, Vol. 76, Iss. 21, p. 121.
11 Jacobius, A. (2003), "Passive, not stupid", *Pensions & Investments*, Chicago, September 1, 2003, Vol. 31, Iss. 18, p. 26.
12 Grene, S., "Fundamentalists struggle to win battle of the indices", *Financial Times Fund Management*, June 23, 2008.
13 Description based on "The rise of absolute return investing", 2009, <http://www.watsonwyatt.com/europe/pubs/globalinvestment/render2.asp?id=15482>.
14 Steve Johnson, S., "130/30 funds falling short of promise", *Financial Times Fund Management*, October 1, 2007, p. 7.
15 <http://www.axarosenberg.com/en/about/profile>. Date accessed: August 11 2009.

16 <http://global.vanguard.com/international/common/pdf/webelieve4_042006.pdf>.
    Date accessed: August 11, 2009.
17 <http://integerethicalfunds.com/IEF_Investment_Pres_Oct2007v1.pdf>. Date accessed:
    August 11, 2009.
18 <http://www.ubs.com/1/e/globalam/gis/gsp.html>. Date accessed: August 11, 2009.
19 <http://www.ubs.com/1/e/globalam/gis/gsp.html>. Date accessed: August 11, 2009.
20 <http://www.axarosenberg.com/en/about/beliefs>. Date accessed: August 11, 2009.
21 <http://www.lapp.ab.ca/invest/SIPG_Dec_07.pdf>. Date accessed: August 23, 2009.

Chapter 6   Risk Premiums

1 "The Yale Endowment 2007", Retrieved from: <http://www.yale.edu/investments/
   Yale_Endowment_07.pdf>.
2 "The Yale Endowment 2008", Retrieved from: <http://www.yale.edu/investments/
   Yale_Endowment_08.pdf>.
3 "The Yale Endowment 2008", Retrieved from: <http://www.yale.edu/investments/
   Yale_Endowment_08.pdf>.
4 "Ivory-towering infernos; Endowments", *The Economist*, Vol. 389, London,
   December 13, 2008, Iss. 8610.
   Arnsdorf, I. (2009, January 26), "Swensen defends 'Yale Model'", *Yale Daily News*.
   Authers, J. (2007, June 9), "A great investor with a centuries-long horizon long
   view", *Financial Times*, London, 16.
5 "The Yale Endowment 2007", Retrieved from: <http://www.yale.edu/invest-
   ments/Yale_Endowment_07.pdf>.
6 "The Yale Endowment 2008", p. 5. Retrieved from: <http://www.yale.edu/invest-
   ments/Yale_Endowment_08.pdf>.
7 "The Yale Endowment 2007". Retrieved from: <http://www.yale.edu/invest-
   ments/Yale_Endowment_07.pdf>.
8 Sender, H. (2007, August. 24), "Deep well: How a Gulf petro-state invests its oil
   riches", *The Wall Street Journal* (Eastern Edition), p. A.1.
   Hettena, S. (2009, February 18), "Yale's financial wizard, David Swensen, says
   most endowments shouldn't try to be like Yale", *ProPublica*.
9 Karmin, C. (2009, January 13), "Yale's investor keeps playbook", *Wall Street
   Journal* (Eastern edition), New York, C.1.
10 Gompers and Lerner (2000), Kaplan and Schoar (2005), Ljungqvist, Richardson,
   and Wolfenzon (2007).
11 Buckman, R. (2007, August 28), "Venture firms vs. investors; Yale and the
   like quietly cite pressure to back offbeat funds", *The Wall Street Journal* (Eastern
   Edition), New York, p. C.1.
12 Arnsdorf, I. (2009, January 26), "Swensen defends 'Yale Model'", *Yale Daily News*.
13 Hettena, S. (2009, February 18), "Yale's financial wizard, David Swensen, says
   most endowments shouldn't try to be like Yale", *ProPublica*.
   <http://www.propublica.org/article/yales-financial-wizard-david-swensen-says-
   most-endowments-shouldnt-try-to-b>.
14 Hettena, S. (2009, February 18), "Yale's financial wizard, David Swensen, says most
   endowments shouldn't try to be like Yale", *ProPublica*. Retrieved from: <http://

www.propublica.org/article/yales-financial-wizard-david-swensen-says-most-endow-ments- shouldnt-try-to-b>.

15 Grene, S. (2008, July 7), "Dealing with the inflation beast", *Financial Times Fund Management*, p. 5. Retrieved from: <http://www.ft.com/cms/s/0/e7b8af3c-4bc1-11dd-a490-000077b07658.html>.
16 <http://www.nzsuperfund.co.nz/files/SIPSP%20p.%206%20-%20230608.pdf>. Date accessed: August 11, 2009.
17 <http://global.vanguard.com/international/common/pdf/webelieve7_042006.pdf>. Date accessed: August 11, 2009.
18 Grene, S. (2007, June 4), "A worrying ignorance of risk", *Financial Times Fund Management*, p. 4. Retrieved from: <http://www.ft.com/cms/s/0/d82a814e-1238-11dc-b963-000b5df10621.html?nclick_check=1>.
19 Skypala, P. (2008, February 4), "Time to get real on pensions", *Financial Times Fund Management*, p. 6.

Chapter 7   Diversification

1 Based on Ibison, D. (2007, June 4), "Norway eludes the oil curse by diversifying into equities", *Financial Times Fund Management*, p. 6. Retrieved from: <http://www.ft.com/cms/s/0/835d79ce-1237-11dc-b963-000b5df10621.html>.
2 2,275 billion dollars at 31-12-2008. Retrieved from: <http://www.norges-bank.no/templates/article____41397.aspx>. Date accessed: May 7, 2009. NBIM.
3 Retrieved from: <http://www.norges-bank.no/templates/article____73432.aspx>. Date accessed: May 7, 2009. NBIM.
4 Stichting Shell Pensioenfonds Feiten & Cijfers 2007, p.8. Retrieved from: <http://www.shell.com/home/content/pensioenfonds-nl/annual_reports/nl/jaarver-slagen.html>. Date accessed: May 7, 2009.
5 Montagu-Smith, N. (2001, October 28), "Boots confirms pension fund move", Telegraph. Retrieved from: <http://www.telegraph.co.uk/finance/personal-finance/2739657/Boots-confirms-pension-fund-move.html>. Date accessed: May 7, 2009.
6 Johnson, S. (2008, November 3), "Safe havens can still be found in the global storms", *Financial Times Fund Management*.
7 <http://www.nzsuperfund.co.nz/files/SIPSP%20p.%206%20-%20230608.pdf>. Date accessed: August 11, 2009.
8 <http://global.vanguard.com/international/common/pdf/webelieve2_042006.pdf>. Date accessed: August 11, 2009.
9 <http://www.uss.co.uk/UssInvestments/Documents/Investment%20Beliefs.pdf>. Date accessed: August 11, 2009.
10 Johnson, S. (2008, November 3), "Safe havens can still be found in the global storm", *Financial Times Fund Management*, p. 3.
11 Rob Taylor, "Australia could delay emissions trade beyond 2010", July 6, 2008, *Reuters*. Retrieved from: <http://www.reuters.com/article/environmentNews/id-USSYD19024120080707>. Date accessed: June 19, 2009.
12 <http://www.investopedia.com/articles/mutualfund/05/HedgeFundHist.asp>.
13 Bram van den Oever (2006, August/September) Spreiden doet lijden, Nederlands Pensioen- & Beleggingsnieuws, augustus/september 2006, Vol. 11, p. 35. Retrieved

from: <http://www.npn-online.com/news/fullstory.php/aid/445/Spreiden_doet_lijden.html>.

14 This example draws on the *Financial Times Fund Management* Section article, December 1, 2008, p. 3.

Chapter 8   Investment Horizon

1 Formally: CNAV (Caisse Nationale d'Assurance Vieillesse) Old Age Fund, the Organic (Caisse de retraite des commerçants et des chefs d'entreprises commerciales) Fund for self-employed retailers and business heads, and the Cancava (Caisse de retraite des artisans) Fund for skilled tradespersons.
2 Yermo, J. (2008), "Governance and investment of public pension reserve funds in selected OECD countries", OECD Working Papers on Insurance and Private Pensions, No. 15, OECD Publishing. doi:10.1787/244270553278.
3 <http://integerethicalfunds.com/IEF_Investment_Pres_Oct2007v1.pdf>. Date accessed: August 11, 2009.
4 <http://global.vanguard.com/international/common/pdf/investmentphilosphy_042006.pdf>. Date accessed: August 11, 2009.
5 <http://www.pggm.nl/About_PGGM/Investments/About_Investments/Investment_philosophy/Investment_philosophy.asp>. Date accessed: August 11, 2009.

Chapter 9   The Investment Process: Impact and Focus of Decisions

1 Deborah Brewster, "Active fund pushes its style to the max", *Financial Times*, London (UK): June 9, 2008, p. 9.
2 Annual Report 2008, <http://70.35.24.107/otpp/ar_08/ar08_highlights.htm>. Date accessed: July 29, 2009.
3 Retrieved   from: <http://www.otpp.com/wps/wcm/connect/otpp_en/Home/Corporate+Info/Annual+Reporting/Annual+Report+and+Results2/>. Date accessed: May 9, 2009.
4 <http://www.otpp.com/wps/wcm/connect/otpp_en/Home/Investments/Investment + Strategy/Investment+Principles/>.
5 "Pupils to teachers", Project Finance, London: September 2007, p. 1, Copyright Euromoney Institutional Investor PLC, September 2007.
6 <http://www.axarosenberg.com/en/about/profile>. Date accessed: August 11, 2009.
7 <https://www2.troweprice.com/rms/marketing/v/index.jsp?vgnextoid=7ed408-d6b6257110VgnVCM100000a18816acRCRD>. Date accessed: August 2009.
8 <http://www.otpp.on.ca/wps/wcm/connect/otpp_en/Home/Investments/Investment+ Strategy/Investment+Principles/>. Date accessed: August 23, 2009.
9 <http://seekingalpha.com/article/24850-is-currency-an-asset-class>.
10 Selling quote from a currency manager: A balanced currency portfolio is true added value to the portfolio. It never happens that *all* currencies depreciate.
11 John Redwood, "Trustees should take asset allocation advice", *Financial Times Fund Management*, October 20, 2008, p. 9. Date accessed: <http://www.ft.com/cms/s/0/e6cf8dec-9c76-11dd-a42e-000077b07658.html?nclick_check=1>.

Chapter 10   Risk Management

1 Ralfe, J. (2003), "The world has moved on, so should pension funds: It is two years since Boots' pension scheme switched out of equities into bond. John Ralfe, who masterminded the transition explains", *Financial Times*, London, October 27, 2003, p. 5.
2 Barry, R. (2001), "Boots finds a safe pension prescription: Investing in equities is out as fund moves assets into bonds, writes Barry Riley", *Financial Times*, London, November 1, 2001, p. 26.
3 Ralfe, J. (2002), "Boots pension move out of equities not about accounting", *Financial Times*, London, January 14, 2002, p. 16.
4 Ralfe, J. (2001), "Rest easy, Boots pensioners", *Financial Times*, London, November 5, 2001, p. 20.
5 Ralfe, J. (2003), "The world has moved on, so should pension funds: It is two years since Boots' pension scheme switched out of equities into bond. John Ralfe, who masterminded the transition explains", *Financial Times*, London, October 27, 2003, p. 5.
6 Ralfe, J. (2003), "The world has moved on, so should pension funds: It is two years since Boots' pension scheme switched out of equities into bond. John Ralfe, who masterminded the transition explains", *Financial Times*, London, October 27, 2003, p. 5.
7 Cohen, N., "Boots pension fund to stay in low-risk bonds", *FT.com*, London, June 20, 2004, p. 1.
8 Anonymous (2002), "Pension funds predicted to keep up pace of equity exodus", *Euroweek*, London, March 4, 2002, Iss. 742, p. 6.
9 Preesman, L. (2009), "Rabobank Pensioenfonds: Riante positie dankzij tijdige hedge", *IPE.com*, January 23, 2009. Retrieved from: <http://www.ipe.com/neder-land/Rabobank_PensioenfondsRiante_positie_dankzij_tijdige_hedge_30468.php>. Date accessed: July 13, 2009.
10 Verklaring inzake de beleggingsbeginselen Stichting Rabobank Pensioenfonds, Retrieved from: <http://www.sprpensioenfonds.nl/Images/20071009%20Verk-laring%20beleggingsbeginselen%20-%20niet%20opgemaakt_tcm83-122255.pdf>, Date accessed: July 10, 2009.
11 Annual Report 2008 Rabobank Pensioenfonds, <http://www.rabobankpensioen-fonds.nl/Images/20090626_Rabobank_Jaarverslag%202008_tcm83-142612.pdf>. Date accessed: July 12, 2009.
12 Annual Report 2008 Rabobank Pensioenfonds, <http://www.rabobankpensioen-fonds.nl/Images/20090626_Rabobank_Jaarverslag%202008_tcm83-142612.pdf>. Date accessed: July 12, 2009.
13 Preesman, L. (2009), "Rabobank Pensioenfonds: Riante positie dankzij tijdige hedge", *IPE.com*, January 23, 2009. Retrieved from: <http://www.ipe.com/neder-land/Rabobank_PensioenfondsRiante_positie_dankzij_tijdige_hedge_30468.php>. Date accessed: July 13, 2009.
14 Preesman, L. (2009), "Hedge change costs Rabo scheme 65% of returns", *IPE.com*, July 16, 2008. Retrieved from: <http://www.ipe.com/news/Hedge_change_costs_Rabo_scheme_65_of_returns_28569.php>. Date accessed: July 2009.
15 Preesman, L. (2009), "Rabobank Pensioenfonds: Riante positie dankzij tijdige hedge", *IPE.com*, January 23, 2009. Retrieved from: <http://www.ipe.com/neder-

land/Rabobank_PensioenfondsRiante_positie_dankzij_tijdige_hedge_30468.php>. Date accessed: July 13, 2009.

16 Shell Pensioenfonds Newsletter March 2009. Retrieved from: <http://www-static. shell.com/static/pensioenfonds-nl/downloads/news_pensfund/newsletters/nws-brief.01_mrt09_web_eng.pdf>. Date accessed: July 13, 2009.

17 <http://www.shell.com/home/content/pensioenfonds-nl/about_shell/nl/finan-cieringsbeleid/dekkingsgraad/dekkingsgraad.html>. Date accessed: July 14, 2009.

18 Quote of Bart van der Steenstraten, Managing Director of SAMCo, the organisation that manages the investments of various Shell pension funds, including the large Shell Pension Fund in the Netherlands from the Shell Pensioenfonds Newsletter April 2009. Retrieved from: <http://www-static.shell.com/static/pensioenfonds-nl/downloads/news_pensfund/newsletters/nwsbrf.02_apr09_web_eng.pdf?. Date accessed: July 13, 2009.

19 <http://www.lapp.ab.ca/invest/SIPG_Dec_07.pdf>. Date accessed: August 11, 2009.

20 <http://www.omers.com/Assets/investments/StatementofInvestmentBeliefs.pdf>. Date accessed: August 11, 2009.

21 <http://www.otpp.on.ca/wps/wcm/connect/otpp_en/home/investments/invest-ment+strategy/risk+management>. Date accessed: August 11, 2009.

22 Example based on Laurens Swinkels, *Minder risico and toch hetzelfde rendement*, NPN, Augustus/September 2008, p. 8.

Chapter 11   Investment Style

1 At March 31 2009; Retrieved from: <http://www.brandes.com/Inv/Pages/AtAGlance. aspx>. Date accessed: May 17, 2009.

2 <http://www.brandes.com/Inv/Pages/PhilosophyAndHistory.aspx>. Date accessed: March 10, 2009.

3 <http://www.brandes.com/Documents/HandoutBrandesFirmHistory.pdf>, "Beginnings: The founding of brandes investment partners" (February 2008). Date accessed: February 24, 2009.

4 <http://www.brandes.com/Documents/HandoutBrandesFirmHistory.pdf>, "Beginnings: The founding of brandes investment partners" (February 2008). Date accessed: February 24, 2009.

5 <http://www.brandes.com/Documents/HandoutBrandesFirmHistory.pdf>, "Beginnings: The founding of brandes investment partners" (February 2008). Date accessed: February 24, 2009.

6 O'Connor, C. (2006, November 13). "Brandes puts muscle behind its bond push", *Pensions & Investments*, Chicago, Vol. 34 (23), p. 6.

7 Pichardo, R. (2008, August 18). "Brandes' performance, outflows give pause", *Pensions & Investments*, Chicago. Vol. 36 (17), p. 6.

8 <http://www.brandes.com/Inv/Pages/AtAGlance.aspx Website Brandes Investment Partners>. Date accessed: March 10, 2009.

9 Pichardo, R. (2008, August 18). "Brandes' performance, outflows give pause", *Pensions & Investments*, Chicago, Vol. 36 (17), p. 6.

10 <http://www.brandes.com/Documents/Handouts/Handout-2008 %20in%20Review%20Crisis%20and%20the%20Rational%20Investor.pdf>, "2008

in review: Fear, crisis, and the rational investor" (January 2009). Date accessed: February 24, 2009.

11 <http://www.brandes.com/Documents/Handouts/Handout-Interview%20with%20Charles%20Brandes%20June%202008.pdf>, "An interview with Charles Brandes" (June 2008).

12 <http://financial-dictionary.thefreedictionary.com/Investment+styles>.

13 Based on Ibison, David, Norway eludes the oil curse by diversifying into equities, *Financial Times Fund Management*, June 4, 2007, p. 6.

14 Coleman M. (2008), "Index funds continue gaining market share vs. active management". Retrieved from: <http://seekingalpha.com/article/66264-index-funds-continue-gaining-market-share-vs-active-management>.

15 William Hall, Jane Martinson, 1999, COMPANIES & FINANCE: UK: UBS revises targets after poor P&D performance, *Financial Times*, January 29, 1999, p. 20.

16 Beleggingsbeginselen ABP; <http://www.abp.nl/abp/abp/images/Verklaring-inzake-Beleggingsbeginslen-ABP-2010N_tcm108-110994.pdf>. Date accessed: September 8, 2010.

17 <http://www.pension.dk/default.asp?id=1052>. Date accessed: August 11, 2009.

18 Steve Johnson, "Magic formula' defies all the rules", *Financial Times Fund Management*, September 15, 2008, p. 3.

19 Retrieved from: <http://www.berkshirehathaway.com/qtrly/1stqtr09.pdf>. Date accessed: May 18, 2009.

20 Michael Russell, *Investing: Top Down or Bottom Up*, September 27, 2007, <http://www.4free-articles.com/finance/investing/investing-top-down-or-bottom-up-.html>.

21 <http://www.nber.org/digest/jun04/w10327.html>.

22 <http://notasheepmaybeagoat.blogspot.com/2008/10/warren-buffett-contrarian-view.html>.

Chapter 12   Costs

1 Skypala, Pauline, (2009), "Hopefully, low-cost model will shine", *Financial Times*, London, March 2, 2009, p. 6.

2 Bogle, J. C. (2006), "Capitalism, entrepreneurship, and investing – The 18th century vs. the 21st century", Speech from John Bogle January 25, 2006, Retrieved from the Bogle Financial Markets Research Center. <http://www.vanguard.com/bogle_site/sp20060125.htm>. Date accessed: June 29, 2009.

3 Stevenson, D. (2009), "Adventurous investor: Why 1 per cent makes all the difference", *FT.com*, London, June 5, 2009.

4 Farzad, R. (2009), "Jack Bogle's last crusade?", *Business Week*, New York, April 20, 2009, Iss. 4127, p. 40.

5 This holds for Dutch pension funds. Research for regarding other countries hint that these cost differences are even larger in a number of other countries. (Bateman, H. and Mitchell, O. S. (2004), "New evidence on pension plan design and administrative expenses: The Australian experience", *Journal of Pension Economics and Finance*, Vol. 3, pp. 63–76; and Dobronogov, A. and Murthi, M. (2005), "Administrative fees and costs of mandatory private pensions in transition economies", *Journal of Pension Economics and Finance*, Vol. 4, pp. 31–55.

6 Bogle, J. C. (1997), "The first index mutual fund: A history of vanguard index trust and the vanguard index strategy", Retrieved from the Bogle Financial Markets Research Center. <http://www.vanguard.com/bogle_site/lib/sp19970401.html>. Date accessed: June 30, 2009.

7 Bogle, J. C. (2006), "Capitalism, entrepreneurship, and investing – The 18th century vs. the 21st century", Speech from John Bogle January 25, 2006, Retrieved from the Bogle Financial Markets Research Center: <http://www.vanguard.com/bogle_site/sp20060125.htm>. Date accessed: June 29, 2009.

8 Bogle, J. C. (2007), "'Value' strategies", *Wall Street Journal* (Eastern Edition), New York, February 9, 2007, p. A.11.

9 Skypala, Pauline (2009), "Hopefully, low-cost model will shine", *Financial Times,* London, March 2, 2009, p. 6.

10 Bogle, J. C. (2006), "Capitalism, entrepreneurship, and investing – The 18th century vs. the 21st century", Speech from John Bogle January 25, 2006, Retrieved from the Bogle Financial Markets Research Center: <http://www.vanguard.com/bogle_site/sp20060125.htm>. Date accessed: June 29, 2009.

11 Coleman, M. (2008), "Index funds continue gaining market share vs. active management", February 27, 2008. Retrieved from: <http://seekingalpha.com/article/66264-index-funds-continue-gaining-market-share-vs-active-management>. Date accessed: July 13, 2009.

12 Bogle, J. C. (2005), "The relentless rules of humble arithmetic", Speech of John Bogle, Retrieved from the Bogle Financial Markets Research Center: <http://www.vanguard.com/bogle_site/sp20060101.htm>. Date accessed: July 1, 2009.

13 Davis, J. (1999), "Focus: The vanguard way to fund management", *The Independent,* May 5, 1999.

14 Davis, J. (2001), "Jonathan Davis: Vanguard shows how structure is the secret of fund success", *The Independent,* May 16, 2001.

15 Bogle, J. C. (1997), "The first index mutual fund: A history of vanguard index trust and the vanguard index strategy", Retrieved from the Bogle Financial Markets Research Center: <http://www.vanguard.com/bogle_site/lib/sp19970401.html>. Date accessed: June 30, 2009.

16 In the Netherlands, the benefits of intergenerational risk sharing and lower operating and investment costs are a crucial argument in the debate (cf. Muralidhar, A. S., 2001, *Innovations in Pension Fund Management*, Stanford University Press, Stanford, California).

17 Graeme Miller, "Funds paying over 50% more investment fees than five years ago", Watson Wyatt press release, February 28, 2008 (See: <http://www.watsonwyatt.com/asia-pacific/news/press.asp?ID=18721>).

18 A recent example of agency costs occurred in the alternative investment industry. Activist hedge funds and private equity investors were accused of developing an aggressive management style that hurt the European economy. This was particularly unsettling for pension funds, and some of them came in a squeeze when the managers targeted the funds' sponsors. Pension funds are hedge funds' and private equity's largest investors, but were not able to influence the managers.

19 Quoted in Pauline Skypala, "Still pulling the wool over our eyes", *Financial Times Fund Management*, March 3, 2008, p. 7, <http://www.ft.com/cms/s/0/8ac0d8a6-e8c3-11dc-913a-0000779fd2ac.html>.

20   Ruth Sullivan, "Time to scrutinize manager charges", *Financial Times Fund Management*, October 20, 2008, p. 8.
21   Pauline Skypala, "No verdict yet in active vs passive debate", *Financial Times Fund Management*, May 19, 2008, p. 6.
22   John Redwood, "Trustees should take asset allocation advice", *Financial Times Fund Management*, October 20, 2008, p. 9,

Chapter 13   Organization

1   Huha, T. (2008, March 3), "With Madonna and Beyonce on board, ABP is making music", *Pensions & Investments*.
2   Press Release ABP, February 20, 2008.
3   Huha, T. (2008, March 3), "With Madonna and Beyonce on board, ABP is making music", *Pensions & Investments*.
4   "Rock and roll returns for ABP" (2007, November 5). *EPN: European Pensions & Investments News*.
5   Andrews, A., "Michael Jackson's death set to boost Dutch pension fund", Telegraph, July 3, 2009. Retrieved from: <http://www.telegraph.co.uk/finance/newsbysector/banksandfinance/5734936/Michael-Jacksons-death-set-to-boost-Dutch-pension-fund.html>, July 28, 2009.
6   Wuijsters, R. (2008), "Innovative investing", presentation held at the Financial Times conference "Getting the most out of alternative investments"; June 5th 2008; http://www.ftbusinessevents.com/ukalternatives08/images/contentpage/ronald%20wuijster.pdf
7   "ABP to take first swing at timberland investments" (2007, January 29). *EPN: European Pensions & Investments News*.
8   ABP Investments – Strategic Investment Plan ABP 2007–2009, p. 6.
9   "ABP to take first swing at timberland investments" (2007, January 29). *EPN: European Pensions & Investments News*; Press Release ABP (2008, June 4) "ABP and PGGM invest 500 million in innovative, clean technology"; Wuijsters, R. (2008), "Innovative investing".
10   Website ABP: 173 billion at December 31, 2008, <http://www.abp.nl/abp/abp/investments/investments/>, March 3 2009.
11   Huha, T. (2008, March 3) "With Madonna and Beyonce on board, ABP is making music", *Pensions & Investments*.
12   <http://www.assetmanagement.hsbc.com/gam/attachments/corp_brouch.pdf>. Date accessed: August 11, 2009.
13   <https://www2.troweprice.com/rms/marketing/v/index.jsp?vgnextoid=36d-0963b52487110VgnVCM1000006be716acRCRD>. Date accessed: August 11, 2009.
14   <http://www.pension.dk/default.asp?id=1052>. Date accessed: August 11, 2009.
15   <http://www.ap1.se/upload/Upphandling/Attachments/RFP%20US%20Small%20Cap%202008%20(Passive).pdf>. Date accessed: August 11, 2009.
16   <http://www.vfmc.vic.gov.au/InvestmentProfile.aspx>. Date accessed: August 11, 2009.
17   <http://www.uss.co.uk/UssInvestments/Documents/Investment%20Beliefs.pdf>. Date accessed: August 11, 2009.
18   <http://www.qic.com/aboutus/default.aspx>.
19   John Plender, "Originative sin", *Financial Times*, January 5, 2009, p. 5.

Chapter 14   Sustainability

1   Stewart, H. (2004), "Long-term life after politics", *The Observer*, November 14, 2004. Retrieved from: <http://www.guardian.co.uk/business/2004/nov/14/theobserver. observerbusiness12>. Date accessed: July 20, 2009.

2   Byrne, F. (2007), "David Blood", *Director*, London, February 2007, Vol. 60, Iss. 7, p. 50. Retrieved from: <http://www.director.co.uk/MAGAZINE/2007/2%20Feb/ blood_60_7.html>. Date accessed: July 20, 2009.

3   Retrieved from: <http://www.generationim.com/strategy/>. Date accessed: July 21, 2009.

4   Stewart, H. (2004), "Long-term life after politics", *The Observer*, November 14, 2004. Retrieved from: <http://www.guardian.co.uk/business/2004/nov/14/theobserver. observerbusiness12>. Date accessed: July 20, 2009.

5   Broadcast transcript of a Radio Interview by Peter Day with Al Gore and David Blood/Global sustainability Programme: Global Business Station: BBC Radio world service (Date: 17/03/2006, Time: 19.05). <http://www.generationim.com/media/ pdf-bbc-david-blood-al-gore-17-03-06.pdf>. Date accessed: July 20, 2004.

6   Broadcast transcript of a Radio Interview by Peter Day with Al Gore and David Blood/Global sustainability Programme: Global Business Station: BBC Radio world service (Date: 17/03/2006, Time: 19.05). <http://www.generationim.com/media/ pdf-bbc-david-blood-al-gore-17-03-06.pdf>. Date accessed: July 20, 2004.

7   Willman, J. (2008), "Never a need to sacrifice returns", *Financial Times*, London, June 3, 2008, p. 6. Retrieved from: <http://www.ft.com/cms/s/0/616021fe-3109-11dd-bc93-000077b07658.html>. Date accessed: July 20, 2009.

8   Tucker, S. (2004), "Gore to invest in issues close to his heart", *Financial Times*, London, November 8, 2004, p. 21. Retrieved from: <http://www.ft.com/cms/s/ 0/560240e0-312a-11d9-a595-00000e2511c8,s01=1.html>. Date accessed: July 20, 2009.

9   Bonaccolta, J. (2007), "When principles aid performance", *Financial Times*, London, May 1, 2007, p. 10. Retrieved from: <http://search.ft.com/ftArticle?queryText= when+principles+aid+performance&y=0&aje=true&x=0&id=070430000706&ct=0>. Date accessed: July 20, 2009.

10 Retrieved from: <http://www.generationim.com/about/mission.html>. Date accessed: July 21, 2009.

11 Willman, J. (2008), "Never a need to sacrifice returns", *Financial Times*, London, June 3, 2008, p. 6. Retrieved from: <http://www.ft.com/cms/s/0/616021fe-3109-11dd-bc93-000077b07658.html>. Date accessed: July 20, 2009.

12 Tucker, S. (2004), "Blood and Gore launch firm with a difference", *Financial Times*, November 8, 2004. <http://www.generationim.com/media/pdf-ft-08-11-04.pdf>. Date accessed: July, 20, 2009.

13 Broadcast transcript of a Radio Interview by Peter Day with Al Gore and David Blood/Global sustainability Programme: Global Business Station: BBC Radio world service (Date: 17/03/2006, Time: 19.05). <http://www.generationim.com/media/ pdf-bbc-david-blood-al-gore-17-03-06.pdf>. Date accessed: July 20, 2004.

14 Willman, J. (2008), "Never a need to sacrifice returns", *Financial Times*, London, June 3, 2008, p. 6. Retrieved from: <http://www.ft.com/cms/s/0/616021fe-3109-11dd-bc93-000077b07658.html>. Date accessed: July 20, 2009.

15　Sucher, S., Beyersdorfer, D. and Jensen, A. D. (2009), Harvard Business School Case: "Generation Investment Management" # 9-609-057, Publication date: March 20, 2009, p. 4.

16　Byrne, F. (2007), "David Blood", *Director*, London, February 2007, Vol. 60, Iss. 7, pp. 50–54. Retrieved from: <http://www.director.co.uk/MAGAZINE/2007/2%20Feb/blood_60_7.html>. Date accessed: July 20, 2009.
Maitland, A. (2006), "Investment for the next generation", *FT.com*, London, April, 3, 2006, p. 1. Retrieved from: <http://www.ft.com/cms/s/0/9ea3b8bc-c358-11da-a381-0000779e2340.html>. Date accessed: July 20, 2009.

17　Anonymous (2008), "Al Gore's fund to close after attracting $5 billion", *The New York Times*, March 11, 2008. Retrieved from: <http://www.nytimes.com/2008/03/11/business/worldbusiness/11iht-gore.4.10942634.html?_r=1>. Date accessed: July 20, 2009.

18　Maitland, A. (2006), "Generation points to dramatic rise in interest sustainable investment: Al Gore and David Blood tell Alison Maitland they have had great success so far in Australia and Europe in attracting investors", *Financial Times*, London, April 3, 2006, p. 10. Retrieved from: <http://www.sbs.ox.ac.uk/NR/rdonlyres/08DE477C-383D-4431-8A91-BC7DCCE65C53/1575/03AprilFT.pdf>. Date accessed: July 20, 2009.

19　Sucher, S., Beyersdorfer, D. and Jensen, A. D. (2009), Harvard Business School Case: "Generation Investment Management" # 9-609-057, Publication date: March 20, 2009, p. 4.

20　Maitland, A. (2006), "Investment for the next generation", *FT.com*, London, April 3, 2006, p. 1. Retrieved from: <http://www.ft.com/cms/s/0/9ea3b8bc-c358-11da-a381-0000779e2340.html>. Date accessed: July 20, 2009.

21　Willman, J. (2008), "Never a need to sacrifice returns", *Financial Times*, London, June 3, 2008, p. 6. Retrieved from: <http://www.ft.com/cms/s/0/616021fe-3109-11dd-bc93-000077b07658.html>. Date accessed: July 20, 2009.

22　Retrieved from: <http://www.mistra.org/download/18.244c2fbe120dce4c6af8000-3899/Annual+Review+2008.pdf>. Date accessed: July 28, 2009.

23　Sucher, S., Beyersdorfer, D. and Jensen, A. D. (2009), Harvard Business School Case: "Generation Investment Management" # 9-609-057, Publication date: March 20, 2009, p. 8.

24　Sucher, S., Beyersdorfer, D. and Jensen, A. D. (2009), Harvard Business School Case: "Generation Investment Management" # 9-609-057, Publication date: March 20, 2009, p. 8.

25　Sophia Grene, "Investors sign up to a better world," *Financial Times Fund Management*, November 3, 2008, p. 1. Retrieved from: <http://www.generationim.com/media/pdf-ft-03-11-08.pdf>.

26　Sam Mamudi, "The rise of the activist shareholder in the US boosts socially responsible investment", *Financial Times Fund Management*, November 5, 2007, p. 12.

27　Pharma Futures 3: Emerging Opportunities; <http://www.sustainability.com/researchandadvocacy/reports_article.asp?id=1658>. Date accessed: July 13, 2009. See also Press release "Collaborative investor engagement enters new era", issued by UK Social Investment Forum, August 5 2003, <http://www.uksif.org/cmsfiles/uksif/uksif-collab-engmt.pdf>. Date accessed: July 13, 2009.

28 <http://www.omers.com/Assets/investments/StatementofInvestmentBeliefs.pdf>. Date accessed: August 11, 2009.

29 <http://www.nzsuperfund.co.nz/files/SIPSP%20p.%206%20-%20230608.pdf>. Date accessed: August 11, 2009.

30 Source: annual report 2008: <https://www.calpers.ca.gov/mss-publication/pdf/ xGIPCN0RsQoyQ_2008%20CAFR(r3).pdf>.

31 <http://www.directorship.com/what-calpers-wants>.

32 <http://hfame.com/abt_our_bsnss.aspx>. Date accessed: August 11, 2009.

33 <http://www.omers.com/Assets/investments/StatementofInvestmentBeliefs.pdf>. Date accessed: August 11, 2009.

34 Sophia Grene, "Investors sign up to a better world", *Financial Times Fund Management*, November 3, 2008, p. 1.

Chapter 16   (Re)engineering Your Own Beliefs

1 Sherden's main thesis is to show how vulnerable we are to false prophets when it comes to predicting and forecasting. His advice to any forecast is informed skepticism where we should ask five questions to assess the validity of the forecast:
   1. Is the forecast based on hard science?
   2. How sound are the methods used to make the projection?
   3. Does the forecaster have credible credentials?
   4. Does the forecaster have a proved track record?
   5. To what extent is my belief in a particular forecast influenced by my own personal beliefs and wishful thinking? (*Source*: European Social Investment Forum, 2008, European SRI Study 2008, Paris).

2 Sangera, S., "Why so many mission statements are mission impossible", *Financial Times*, July 22, 2005, p. 8.

3 Directive 2003/41/EC of the European Parliament and of the Council, of 3 June 2003, on the activities and supervision of institutions for occupational retirement provision. Paragraph 23 mentions that: "The investment policy of an institution is a decisive factor for both security and affordability of occupational pensions. The institutions should therefore draw up and, at least every three years, review a statement of investment principles. It should be made available to the competent authorities and on request also to members and beneficiaries of each pension scheme."

4 See Klamer (2007) and McCloskey (1990) for more information about story-telling. This is especially relevant for investment consultants and analysts; creating a good story is interpreted as a convincing one.

5 Paul Trickett, "Governance key to dynamic investing", *Financial Times Fund Management*, December 3, 2007.

References

Aggarwal, R., I. Erel, R. M. Stulz, and R. G. Williamson, 2007, "Do U.S. firms have the best corporate governance? A cross-country examination of the relation between corporate governance and shareholder wealth" (January 2007). Fisher College of Business Working Paper No. 2006-03-006; ECGI – Finance Working Paper No. 145/2007; Charles A. Dice Center Working Paper No. 2006-25. Available at SSRN: http://ssrn.com/abstract=954169

Alexander, J. C., S. W. Barnhart, and S. Rosenstein, 2007, "Do investor perceptions of corporate governance initiatives affect firm value: The case of TIAA-CREF", *The Quarterly Review of Economics and Finance* 47, 198–214.

Ambachtsheer, K., 2004, "Should (could) you manage your fund like Harvard or Ontario Teachers?", *The Ambachtsheer Letter.*

——, 2005, "Key workshop findings and conclusions", *ICPM Conference Investment Beliefs, Risk, and Pension Fund Governance*, October 2005.

——, 2007, *Pension Revolution. A Solution to the Pensions Crisis*, John Wiley & Sons.

——, 2009, "Scale in pension fund management: Does it matter?", *The Ambachtsheer Letter* #280, KPA Advisory Services Ltd., Toronto.

Ambachtsheer, K., R. Capelle, and H. Lum, 2006, "Pension fund governance today: Strengths, weaknesses, and opportunities for improvement", *Financial Analysts Journal*, October 2006.

——, 2007, "The state of global pension fund governance today: Board competency still a problem", Rotman International Centre for Pension Management.

Ambachtsheer, K., R. Capelle, and Scheibelbut, 1998, "Improving pension fund performance", *Financial Analysts Journal* 15–21.

Ambachtsheer, K., and D. Ezra, 1994, *Pension Fund Excellence*, Wiley, New York.

Anson, M., 2005, "Institutional portfolio management", *Journal of Portfolio Management.*

Arnott, R. D., J. Hsu, and P. Moore, 2005, "Fundamental indexing", *Financial Analysts Journal* 61, 83–99.

Baker, N., and R. Haugen, 1991, "The efficient market inefficiency of capitalization-weighted stock portfolios", *Journal of Portfolio Management* 17, 35–40.

Bartlema, S., 2005, "Heineken reaches the parts other beers cannot reach", *2005 Euro Investment Workshop*, Amsterdam.

Bauer, R., and R. G. Frehen, 2008, *The Performance of US Pension Funds*, SSRN.

Behr, P., A. Guttler, and F. Miebs, 2008, "Is minimum-variance investing really worth the while? An analysis with robust performance inference", Working Paper.

Beinhocker, E. D., 2006, "The adaptable corporation", *McKinsey Quarterly.*

Berkelaar, A. B., M. Tsumagari, and A. Kobor, 2006, "The sense and nonsense of risk budgeting", *Financial Analysts Journal* 62, 63–75.

Berkowitz, S. A., L. D. Finney, and D. E. Logue, 1988, *The Investment Performance of Corporate Pension Plans*, Quorom Books, New York.

Bikker, J. A., and J. De Dreu, 2007, "Operating costs of pension funds: The impact of scale, governance, and plan design", *Journal of Pension Economics and Finance.*

Blake, D., B. N. Lehmann, and A. Timmermann, 1999, "Asset allocation dynamics and pension fund performance", *The Journal of Business* 72, 429–461.

Bodie, Z., 1995, "On the risk of stocks in the long run", *Financial Analysts Journal*, 18–22.

Boeri, T., L. Bovenberg, B. Coeuré, and A. Roberts, 2006, *Dealing with the New Giants: Rethinking the Role of Pension Funds*, International Center for Monetary and Banking Studies (ICMB), Geneva.

Bogle, J. C., 2008, "A question so important that it should be hard to think about anything else", *Journal of Portfolio Management* 95–102.

Boston University, 2009, "Paul Samuelson and Robert Merton differ on the causes of the financial crisis", http://www.youtube.com/watch?v=zCudGmRIsfk.

Brav, A., and J. B. Heaton, 2001, *Competing Theories of Financial Anomalies*, SSRN.

Brinson, G. P., L. R. Hood, and G. L. Beebower, 1986, "Determinants of portfolio performance", *Financial Analysts Journal* 39–44.

Brinson, G. P., L. B. D. Singer, and G. L. Beebower, 1991, "Determinants of portfolio performance II: An update", *Financial Analysts Journal*.

Campbell, R. A., K. G. Koedijk, and P. Kofman, 2002, *Increased Correlation in Bear Markets: A Downside Risk Perspective*, SSRN.

Chevalier, J., and G. Ellison, 1999, "Are some mutual fund managers better than others? Cross-sectional patterns in behavior and performance", *Journal of Finance* 54, 875–899.

Chua, D., M. Kritzman, and S. Page, 2008, "The myth of diversification", *The Journal of Portfolio Management* 36, 26–35.

Clark, G. L., E. Caerlewy-Smith, and J. C. Marshall, 2006, "Pension fund trustee competence: Decision making in problems relevant to investment practice", *Journal of Pension Economics and Finance* 5, 91–110.

Clark, G. L., and T. Hebb, 2004, "Pension fund corporate engagement: The fifth stage of capitalism", *Relations industrielles* 59, 142–171.

Clark, G. L., and R. Urwin, 2007, *Best-Practice Investment Management: Lessons for Asset Owners from the Oxford-Watson Wyatt Project on Governance*, Oxford University for the Environment, Oxford.

——, 2008, "Best-practice pension fund management", *Journal of Asset Management* 9, 2–21.

Clarke, R., and S. Thorley, 2006, "Minimum-variance portfolios in the U.S. equity market", *Journal of Portfolio Management* 33, 10–24.

Collins, J., 2001, *Good To Great*, Random House Business Books, London.

Cooper, S., and D. Bianco, 2003, "Should pension funds invest in equities?", *Q-Series: Pension Fund Asset Allocation*, UBS Investment Research, London.

Culp, C. L., 2001, *The Risk Management Process*, John Wiley & Sons, Inc., New York.

Damodaran, A., 2007, "Investment philosophy: The secret ingredient in investment success", http://pages.stern.nyu.edu/~adamodar/pdfiles/invphiloh/ invphilintro.pdf.

Davis, E. P., and B. Steil, 2004, *Institutional Investors*, MIT Press, Cambridge, MA.

De Bondt, W. F. M., and R. H. Thaler, 1985, "Does the stock market overreact?", *Journal of Finance* 40, 793–805.

De Graaf, F. J., and A. Slager, 2009, "Guidelines for integrating socially responsible investment in the investment process", *Journal of Investing* 18, 70–78.

DeLong, J. B., and K. Magin, 2009, "The U.S. equity return premium: Past, present, and future", *The Journal of Economic Perspectives* 23, 193–208.

Denison, D., 2008, "Know thyself: What Canada's pension plans can learn from each other", Notes for Remarks to Pension Investment Association of Canada Spring Conference May 8, 2008.

Derwall, J., N. Guenster, R. Bauer, and K. Koedijk, 2005, "The eco-efficiency premium puzzle", *Financial Analysts Journal* 61, 51–64.

Derwall, J., K. Koedijk and J. Ter Horst, 2010, "A tale of values-driven and profit-seeking social investors", Working Paper.

Dimson, E., P. Marsh, and M. Staunton, 2003, "Global evidence on the equity risk premium", *Journal of Applied Corporate Finance* 15, 27–38.

——, 2006, "The worldwide equity premium: A smaller puzzle", London Business School.

Dreman, D., and M. Berry, 1995, "Overreaction, underreaction and the low P/E effect", *Financial Analysts Journal* 21–30.

Economist, The, 2008, "All bets are off", *The Economist*.

Ellison, R., and A. Jolly, 2008, *The Pension Trustee's Investment Guide*, Thorogood Publishing Ltd., London.

——, 2009, *The Pension Trustee's Investment Guide*, Thorogood Publishing Ltd.

Emek, B., 2004, "Selling a cheaper mousetrap: Wal-Mart's effect on retail prices", Department of Economics, University of Missouri.

Engstrom, S., R. Grottheim, P. Norman, and C. Ragnartz, 2008, *Alpha-Beta-Separation: From Theory to Practice*, SSRN.

Fabozzi, F. J., J. N. Gordon, and S. Hudson-Wilson, 2005, "Why real estate?", *The Journal of Portfolio Management* 12–27.

Fama, E. F., 1970, "Efficient capital markets: A review of theory and empirical work", *The Journal of Finance* 25, 383–417.

Fisher, K. L., and M. Statman, 1999, "A behavioral framework for time diversification", *Financial Analysts Journal* 55, 88–97.

Freeman, A., 2006, *All You Need to Know About Being a Pension Fund Trustee*, Longtail Publishing Limited, London.

Fuller, R. J., 1998, "Behavioral finance and the sources of alpha", *Journal of Pension Plan Investing* 2.

Gallagher, D. R., 2003, "Investment manager characteristics, strategy, top management changes and fund performance", *Accounting and Finance* 43, 283–309.

Ghilarducci, T., 1994, "U.S. pension investment policy and perfect capital market theory", *Challenge* 4–10.

Ghysels, E., P. Santa-Clara, and R. I. Valkanov, 2005, "There is a risk-return tradeoff after all!", *Journal of Financial Economics* 76, 509–548.

Graham, B., and D. L. Dodd, 1951, *Security Analysis: Principles and Technique, 3rd ed*, McGraw-Hill, New York.

Graham, J. R., and C. R. Harvey, 2007, *The Equity Risk Premium in January 2007: Evidence from the Global CFO Outlook Survey*, SSRN.

Grantham, J., 2009, "Obama and the Teflon men, and other short stories, Part 1", *Quarterly Letter, Part 1 – January 2009*, GMO.

Gray, J., 1997, "Overquantification", *Financial Analysts Journal* 53, 5–12.

Greer, R. J., 1997, "What is an asset class anyway?", *The Journal of Portfolio Management*.

Gupta, P., and J. Straatman, 2005, *Skill Based Investment Management*, SSRN.

Gurley, J. W., 2001, "Why Dell's war isn't dumb", *Fortune*.

Guyatt, D., 2005, A summary of the findings of a survey into: "Investment beliefs relating to corporate governance and corporate responsibility", prepared for the Marathon Club, http://www.rotman.utoronto.ca/icpm/files/ Survey%20Summary_ Danyelle%20Guyatt.pdf

——, 2008, "Pension collaboration: Strength in numbers", *Rotman International Journal of Pension Management* 1, 46–52.

Hamel, G., and C. K. Prahalad, 1994, *Competing for the Future*, Harvard Business School Press, Boston, Mass.

Haugen, R. A., 2003, *The New Finance: Overreaction, Complexity and Uniqueness* (3rd edition), Prentice Hall.

Hua, T., 2008, "More pension funds embracing 'alternative beta'", PI Online.

Kentucky Public Pension Working Group, 2008, Strategic Investment and Governance Review; Final Recommendations Hammond Associates, St. Louis.

Koedijk, Kees C. G., and A. Slager, 2009, "Do institutional investors have sensible investment beliefs?", *Rotman International Journal of Pension Management*, Vol. 2, No. 1, 2009. Available at SSRN: http://ssrn.com/abstract=1408662

Koedijk, Kees C. G., A. Slager, and R. Bauer, *Investment Beliefs that Matter: New Insights into the Value Drivers of Pension Funds* (May 8, 2010). Available at SSRN: <http://ssrn.com/abstract=1603262>.

Koijen, R., J. H. Van Binsbergen, and M. W. Brandt, 2008, "Optimal decentralized investment management", *Journal of Finance* 63, 1849–1895.

Kritzman, M. P., 2002, *Puzzles of Finance: Six Practical Problems and Their Remarkable Solutions*, John Wiley & Sons, Inc., New York.

Laboul, A., and J. Yermo, 2006, "Regulatory principles and institutions", in G. L. Clark, A. H. Munnell, and J. M. Orszag (eds), *The Oxford Handbook of Pensions and Retirement Income*, Oxford University Press, Oxford.

Lamoureux, C., 2008, "Effective pension governance: The Ontario teachers' story", *Rotman International Journal of Pension Management* 1, 6–10.

Lerner, J., A. Schoar, and J. Wang, 2008, "Secrets of the academy: The drivers of university endowment success", *Journal of Economic Perspectives* 22, 207–222.

Lo, A. W., 2005, "Reconciling efficient markets with behavioural finance: The adaptive markets hypothesis", *Journal of Investment Consulting* 7, 21–44.

Lo, A. W., and P. N. Patel, 2007, *130/30: The New Long-Only*, SSRN.

Louche, C., and S. Lydenberg, 2006, "Socially responsible investment: Differences between Europe and United States", Vlerick Leuven Gent Management School.

Malkiel, B., 2003, "The efficient market hypothesis and its critics", *Journal of Economic Perspectives* 17, 59–82.

Markowitz, H. M., 1970, *Portfolio Selection: Efficient Diversification of Investments*, Yale University Press, New Haven; London.

McCloskey, D. M., 1990, *If You're So Smart. The Narrative of Economic Expertise*, The University of Chicago Press, Chicago.

McQuarrie, E. F., 2008, "Fundamentally indexed or fundamentally misconceived: Locating the source of RAFI outperformance", *The Journal of Investing* 17, 29–37.

Mercer, 2007, "Planning to address environmental, social and corporate governance issues? What's best practice?", *Multi-employer Superannuation: Newsletter*, March 2007.

Merton, R. C., 2009, "The financial crisis: Challenges and opportunities", *van Lanschot Lecture 2009*, Tilburg University.

Minahan, J. R., 2006, "The role of investment philosophy in evaluating investment managers: A consultant's perspective on distinguishing Alpha from noise", *The Journal of Business* 6–11.

——, 2008, "Evaluating active managers: The role of belief systems", *Advisor Perspectives*.

Minor, D. B., 2007, "Finding the [financial] cost of socially responsible investing", *Journal of Investing* 16, 54–70.

Mintzberg, H., J. B. Quinn, and S. Ghoshal, 1995, *The Strategy Process* (European edition), Prentice Hall International (UK) Limited, Hemel Hempstead.

Mitchell, O. S., and P.-L. Hsin, 1997a, "Managing public sector pensions", in J. Shoven and S. Schieber (eds), *Public Policy Toward Pensions*, MIT Press, Cambridge, MA.

——, 1997b, "Public sector pension governance and performance", in S. V. Prieto (ed.), *The Economics of Pensions: Principles, Policies, and International Experience*, Cambridge University Press, Cambridge.

Morrell, L. R., 2006, "A more effective investment committee: There's a better way to meet challenges facing these teams", University Business.

Morris, M. W., O. J. Sheldon, D. R. Ames, and M. J. Young, 2007, "Metaphors and the market: Consequences and preconditions of agent and object metaphors in stock market commentary", *Organizational Behavior and Human Decision Processes* 102, 174–192.

Muralidhar, A. S., 2001, *Innovations in Pension Fund Management*, Stanford University Press, Stanford, California.

Muralidhar, A. S., and K. Asad-Syed, 2001, "Asset-liability value at risk", in A. S. Muralidhar (ed.), *Innovations in Pension Fund Management*, Stanford University Press, Stanford, California.

Nelson, J. M., 2006, "The 'CalPERS effect' revisited again", *Journal of Corporate Finance* 12, 187–213.

Palme, M., A. Sunden, and P. Soderlind, 2005, "Investment choice in the Swedish premium pension plan", Center for Retirement Research at Boston College, Chestnut Hill, MA.

Peters, T. J., and R. H. Waterman, 1982, *In Search of Excellence*, Harper & Row, Publishers, Inc., New York.

Picerno, J., 1998, *Bull Market*, Dow Jones Asset Management.

Porter, M. E., 1985, *Competitive Advantage*, The Free Press, New York.

Rajan, A., B. Martin, and J. Shaw, 2006, "Tomorrow's products for tomorrow's clients: Innovation imperatives in global asset management", Create Research, Tunbridge Wells.

Rao, D. N., 2007, *Analyzing Style Biases and Performance of Funds*, SSRN eLibrary, SSRN.

Raymond, D., 2008, "Investment beliefs", in F. J. Fabozzi (ed.), *Handbook of Finance: Investment Management and Financial Management*, John Wiley & Sons.

Reinhart, C. M., and K. Rogoff, 2009, "This time is different: Eight centuries of financial folly", Princeton University Press, Princeton and Oxford.

Roberts, J. D., 2004, *The Modern Firm*, Oxford University Press, Oxford.

Russell, C., 2006, *Trustee Investment Strategy for Endowments and Foundations*, John Wiley & Sons, Ltd., Chichester.

Sharpe, W. F., 1994, "The Sharpe ratio", *The Journal of Portfolio Management* 21, 49–58.

Shefrin, H., 2000, *Beyond Greed and Fear*, Harvard Business School Press, Boston, Massachusetts.

Shefrin, H., and M. Statman, 1994, "Behavioral capital asset pricing theory", *Journal of Finance and Quantitative Analysis* 29, 323–349.

Sherden, W. A., 1998, *The Fortune Sellers*, John Wiley & Sons, Inc., New York.

Shiller, R., 2003, "From efficient markets theory to behavioral finance", *Journal of Economic Perspectives* 17, 83–104.

Slager, A. M. H., and K. Koedijk, 2007, "Investment beliefs", *Journal of Portfolio Management* 77–84.

Smith, H., 2008, "Time to fight for fairer deal on fees", *FT Mandate*.

Smith M., 1996, "Shareholder activism by institutional investors: Evidence from CalPERS", *Journal of Finance* 51, 227–252.

Stewart, F., and J. Yermo, 2008, "Pension fund governance: Challenges and potential solutions", Working Papers on Insurance and Private Pensions, No. 18, OECD publishing.

Swensen, D. F., 2000, *Pioneering Portfolio Management – An Unconventional Approach to Institutional Investing*, The Free Press, New York.

Taleb, N. N., 2005, *Fooled by Randomness: The Hidden Role of Chance in Life and in the Markets* (2nd updated edition), Random House.

Tversky, A., and D. Kahneman, 1974, "Judgment under Uncertainty: Heuristics and Biases", *Science* 185, 1124–1131.

Vittas, D., G. Impavido, and R. O'Connor, 2008, *Upgrading the Investment Policy Framework of Public Pension Funds*, SSRN.

Ware, J. W., 2008a, "Applied behavioral finance: From theory to practice", Focus Consulting Group, Inc., Long Grove, Illinois.

——, 2008b, "Investment process review", Focus Consulting Group.

Waring, M. B., and L. B. Siegel, 2006, "The myth of the absolute return-investor", *Financial Analysts Journal* 62, 14–21.

Warwick, B., 2000, *Searching for Alpha*, John Wiley & Sons, Inc., New York.

Watson Wyatt Worldwide, 2005, Global Investment Review, London.

Wright, C., P. Banerjee, and V. R. Boney, 2008, "Behavioral finance: Are the disciples profiting from the doctrine?", *The Journal of Investing* 17, 82–90.

Wuijster, R., 2008, "The Dutch perspective. What are they doing differently?", Presentation at the FT June 5th 2008 Event, London.

Index

.

The manufacturer's authorised representative in the EU is Springer
Nature Customer Service Centre GmbH, Europaplatz 3, 69115 Heidelberg,
Germany. If you have any concerns regarding our products, please
contact ProductSafety@springernature.com

Printed and bound by CPI Group (UK) Ltd, Croydon, CR0 4YY
23/04/2026
02095595-0017